"As a long-term voice of and for youth ministry, Mark Oestreicher has done what few leaders at his level allow themselves to do: Change. This manifesto represents a long-brewing unsettling inside of the president of Youth Specialties. He has listened hard, thought carefully, and let himself be pushed around by new thoughts, ideas, perspectives, and convictions. In *Youth Ministry 3.0*, Marko lets us in on where this process has taken him. As the nature of adolescence as shifted and as careful study has been overshadowed by populist expertise, this book slows us all down enough to help us remember that ministry to kids belongs to Jesus, and not to us. Well done, and thank you."

-Chap Clark, Ph.D., vice dean for the School of Theology and Regional Campuses Master's Programs, Professor of Youth, Family, and Culture, Fuller Theological Seminary

"My first contact with *Youth Ministry 3.0* was when Marko read me a short excerpt to punch up a point he was making during a lively dialogue. I was immediately sure that this book would contribute something unique and provocative to contemporary conversations about youth ministry. Marko is a gifted writer with a sharp eye for detail, a well-stamped passport testifying to a worldwide perspective, and a network of future-thinking power brokers—I can't imagine seriously considering the direction and practice of youth ministry without engaging this book."

-Dave Rahn, Ph.D., chief ministry officer, Youth for Christ/USA

"I finished reading this book in one sitting—I couldn't stop. My palms were sweaty. My eyes filled with tears at different points. My heart raced. I felt a deep sense of 'yes' from the Holy Spirit. *Youth Ministry 3.0* is a prophetic voice to the church. In it are conversations we're having almost on a daily basis. It's validating. It gives us something in writing that we've just been talking about. It gives us language for some things we've had no idea how to express. And, in my opinion, this isn't just a youth ministry book. It's a CHURCH book."

—April Diaz, Next Gen pastor, Newsong Church

"What Mark Oestreicher has done in *Youth Ministry 3.0* is profound. Both historic and prophetic, he shows us where modern American student ministry has been and where it should go. As readers, we're in capable hands with Marko at the wheel, and he steers us (and youth ministry) in a wonderful and needed new direction. This book is a bellwether of youth ministry's future."

—Tony Jones, author of *The New Christians: Dispatches from the Emergent Frontier*

MARK OESTREICHER
FOREWORD BY KENDA CREASY DEAN

YOUTH MINISTRY 3.0

ᴬMANIFESTO

OF WHERE WE'VE BEEN, WHERE WE ARE, AND WHERE WE NEED TO GO

ZONDERVAN®

ZONDERVAN.com/
AUTHORTRACKER
follow your favorite authors

youth
specialties

 youth
specialties

Youth Ministry 3.0: A Manifesto of Where We've Been, Where We Are, and Where We Need to Go
Copyright 2008 by Mark Oestreicher

Youth Specialties resources, 300 S. Pierce St., El Cajon, CA 92020 are published by Zondervan, 5300 Patterson Ave. SE, Grand Rapids, MI 49530.

ISBN 978-0-310-66866-4

Cover design by David Conn
Interior design by Brandi Etheredge Design

Printed in the United States of America

08 09 10 11 12 13 14 • 19 18 17 16 15 14 13 12 11 10 9 8 7 6 5 4 3 2 1

This book is dedicated to the fantastic youth workers who allow Youth Specialties to serve them every year. I'm so humbled and honored to come alongside you, dream with you, cry with you, laugh with you, complain with you, strategize with you, hope with you, and forge ahead with you.

ACKNOWLEDGMENTS

I've written or contributed to a small shelf of books over the years. But in many ways, I feel like this is my first "real" book. Not to demean the others, but this is the first one with real sentences and paragraphs of ideas, written for adults. And, of course, it wasn't written in a vacuum—many added to it.

When I was incubating these ideas for a General Session talk at the National Youth Workers Convention in the fall of 2007, I posted some questions on my blog. A handful of youth workers were especially helpful with suggesting words to describe what I was thinking about in regard to *Youth Ministry 3.0*. Particular thanks go to D. Scott Miller, Chad Swanzy, Joe Troyer, Adam Lehman, Len Evans, Gordon Weir, Tammy Klassen, Jay Phillippi, Natalie Stadnick, Grahame Knox, Dustin Perkins, Sue Van Stelle, Bob Carlton, Tash McGill, Liz Graves, Tammy Harris, Mark Riddle, Robin Dugall, Daniel So, and Jodi Shay.

At the first convention that year, I sat on my hotel balcony for hours with my friend (and YS publisher) Jay Howver, and he helped me flesh out many of my ideas for the application section, which, later, become the seeds for Chapter 6 in this book.

Four very, very smart friends of mine read the first draft of this book and provided extremely helpful and shaping input. After their responses I rewrote entire sections, added new stuff, clarified, and cut. They deserve coauthor credit in many ways. So, big, massive thanks to Dr. Chap Clark, Dr. Kara Powell, almost-Dr. Tony Jones, and Dr. Kenda Creasy Dean.

Michelle Fockler let me use her house for three days as a writing haven. Those three days made all the difference, and I'm in Michelle's debt. Later, I spent two days on revisions in the quiet apartment of my friend Andy Padgen. Dude, perfect writing spot.

Finally, my wife (Jeannie) and kids (Liesl and Max) are the best family this guy could have. I'm so in love with you all, and love my life with you. Thanks for supporting me in this little book.

CONTENTS

Back before Shia LaBeouf was...well...buff, he was a child actor digging in the dirt in *Holes*. The latter is a quirky movie from 2003 drawn from a quirkier novel that almost everybody seems to read in middle school these days, a kind of 21st-century *Lord of the Flies* in which misunderstood youngsters in a draconian juvenile detention facility dig holes all day, every day, for no apparent reason.[1]

It's wildly entertaining fiction, of course—but barely. Scene change: We're now off the coast of Cape Town, South Africa, touring Robben Island, the infamous prison that held anti-apartheid activists such as former South African President and Nobel Peace Prize-winner Nelson Mandela during what South Africans modestly call "the Struggle."[2] I'm privileged to speak with a former inmate who spent his late teens and twenties in this prison. According to my guide, most of the inmates were like him, young and black or "colored" (usually of mixed race or Indian descent). The guards—young, white soldiers also in their late teens or early twenties—were ordered to keep them busy in the lime quarry, great gravel pits where (you guessed it) they dug holes.

My guide worked alongside Mandela during those years, moving gravel from one hole in the ground to another—and then back again. As it turns out, the gravel didn't need moving. No one needed it or used it. Moving gravel in the lime quarry was simply a way to keep the inmates occupied, day after day, year after year. Young black and "colored" prisoners moved gravel back and forth, while young white and free soldiers kept watch.

Here's where it gets interesting. Mandela, 20 years older than most of the prisoners, was a product of a Christian school, where Methodist missionaries instilled in him a passion for liberation and a generous view of divine grace and forgiveness. So Mandela began to see the gravel pits as a school. While moving gravel from one side of the pit to another, Mandela and his colleagues taught each other everything they knew. Mandela taught his young fellow prisoners the contents of his missionary education: Shakespeare and the Bible, English poets and philosophy, the ancient Bantu wisdom *umuntu ngumuntu ngabantu* ("we are people through other people") and Jesus' and Gandhi's views on reconciliation. Mandela fervently believed in the power of education for social change, and at "Robben Island University," as it came to be called, Mandela arranged secret lectures and informal seminars about humanity's interdependence and taught that "the common ground is greater and more enduring than the differences that divide."[3]

Then my guide shared one more remarkable memory. Mandela often purposely taught within earshot of the young white guards. "They were boys as well," said my guide, "and their privilege came through no choice of their own. Mandela believed that they were victims of the same political system that we were. He wanted them to have this education, too."

What do *Holes* and Robben Island have to do with *Youth Ministry 3.0*? Well, let me ask you this: How often have you wondered if the work you're doing in youth ministry is making any difference? Has your church ever kept young people busy, moving gravel from one side of the sanctuary to the other, rearranging ecclesial landfills without substantively changing either young people or the church? Have you ever wondered if the mission trip really mattered—the one where the 10th graders spent all week moving massive rocks to build a wall for an Appalachian family, only to be told by the staff the next day that "they made a mistake," and the wall needed to come down? (That really happened on my church's youth mission trip two weeks ago.) How about your hard-earned training, your long hours at the church, your earnest efforts to help teenagers recognize Jesus Christ's presence? Is God getting through? Are you creating cracks for divine grace, or are you moving gravel, day after day, year after year, for no apparent reason?

Incredibly, Nelson Mandela made a ministry—one that changed the world at the end of the 20th century—out of a lime quarry pit. And what allowed him to transform a futile situation with young people into a faith-inspired, world-changing opportunity for witness? That's what Mark Oestreicher wants to know, too. You're about to open some of the most honest pages written about youth ministry in the last 30 years. With humbling and often hilarious transparency, "Marko" (as the world knows him) names the elephant in the room of youth ministry: "The way we're doing things is *already not working*. We are failing at our calling. And deep down, most of us know it."

Perhaps these are the growing pains we asked for 20 years ago, when we said we wanted youth ministry to be acknowledged as a Christian vocation, and when we begged youth leaders to drop the Mary Poppins act and stay put, even after the wind changes, to see young people through years instead of months of growing up. The areas of children's, youth, and young adult ministries have matured exponentially in the past generation, and those of us in ministry with young people today are better prepared, better paid, and consequently "longer lasting" than ever before.

So the self-doubt we're experiencing may not be "failure" at our callings so much as the vocational equivalent of living longer; the older you get, the more likely you are to experience problems associated with aging. (And isn't aging usually better than the alternative?) The truth is that, until recently, most of us didn't remain in youth ministry long enough to know whether our ministries were really "working" or not. No wonder youth ministry has taken a more serious, theological turn in the 21st century. For the first time, we're looking back over long-term ministries and really trying to answer why, after giving it all we've got, so many of the young people we love don't love Jesus, and why even those who do often confuse him with, say, Oprah or Michael Caine.[4] Theological discernment of our mission and practices for the particular cultural reality we're in is the only responsible way forward. Oestreicher resets our cultural compasses with a perceptive look at how we got here—and why our dominant ideas of what matters to teenagers need to change.

What we must do as youth ministers is what Nelson Mandela did as a prisoner at Robben Island: Discern the best way to use the times we're in to prepare young people to live in the world differently than most, as disciples of Jesus Christ. We may not be able to stop youth ministry from moving gravel back and forth, figuratively speaking, at least not at first—though eventually we must climb out of the lime quarry and onto the road.

But we can certainly start to share with each other everything we've learned, and to do it where young people who're keeping an eye on us can eavesdrop.

I'm humbled by the pages you're about to read. (I'm humbled by anybody who can write a provocative essay without it bloating into a dissertation).[5] *Youth Ministry 3.0* is a painfully honest little book. But Marko is also an exceedingly generous human being; he identifies the problem—that youth ministry misunderstands the fundamental cultural dynamics that engulf young people—without malice or blame, and with a good deal of self-effacement. Once upon a time we called this the virtue "Christian humility," and pastoral literature needs more of it.

But Marko doesn't stop there. He then boldly assumes the role of cultural interpreter, positing a fresh way to think about a culture informed by the assumptions of cellular technology, and by the values of what MIT media guru Henry Jenkins calls "participatory culture." Belonging—or "affinity"—is now the ascendant task of adolescence, believes Marko (I am inclined to believe he's on to something; developmental research seems to be pushing in this direction). "Affinity," he writes, "has become the pathway...to identity formation and autonomy."

Of course, hasn't the Christian story always been more about affinity than autonomy (which Western views of identity formation assume)? Haven't Christians always been a "people," not a person—a body with interdependent parts, equally vital for mission and communion, the work that Christ needs us to do? Here Oestreicher shows his theological hand, gloriously. Then he does what he does best: He lands the plane. Somewhat in spite of himself, he proposes a method of practical reason (see page 110; baptize this and a method of practical theology will suddenly appear) that paints a convincing outline of Youth

Ministry 3.0, ministry that's predicated on mission and communion—in other words, ministry that looks like the church.

Mark Oestreicher is many things: A devout man of faith, a winsome storyteller, a daring thinker, a doting dad and husband, an eager listener, and a very smart guy (read his blog). But the word that came to my mind again and again as I read these pages was *thoughtful*. Mark Oestreicher is one of the most thoughtful leaders in the church today, a man who tirelessly pokes around for God, who's capable of entertaining a guest or an idea as well as a room full or junior high kids or an arena full of youth workers, who's profoundly impressed by Jesus Christ without being impressed with himself. He offers these pages as thoughts, not solutions—as a sign pointing out of the gravel pit.

I'm going to follow it and see where it goes.

Kenda Creasy Dean
Princeton, New Jersey
August 2008

---

[1]Louis Sachar, *Holes* (New York: Farrar, Straus and Giroux, 1998). Sachar's book won the prestigious Newberry Medal for excellence in children's literature in 1999.

[2]Mandela spent 27 years here before his release in 1990. When I asked my guide why he and his young, strong friends didn't try to escape by swimming across the inlet to Cape Town, my guide simply said: "Sharks."

[3]See Nelson Mandela, *Long Walk to Freedom: The Autobiography of Nelson Mandela* (Austin, TX: Holt, Rinehart and Winston, 2000). For a thoughtful

 14

summary of Mandela's influences as an educator, including "Robben Island University," see Anders Hallengren, "Nelson Mandela and the Rainbow of Culture," (September 11, 2001) http://nobelprize.org/nobel_prizes/peace/articles/mandela/index.html (accessed August 9, 2008). Hallengren points out that, given the fact that prisoners came from a multitude of religious backgrounds (only a few inmates on Robben Island were Christians), Shakespeare–not the Bible–gave inmates their unifying language. Still, Mandela himself took great pains to credit Christianity as the inspiration for his life's work and vision of reconciliation (his mother was a devout Christian and was responsible for his missionary schooling). During his years in prison, progovernment sources consistently portrayed Mandela as a godless infidel. He consistently repudiated this. Passionately crediting religion's decisive importance in South Africa's liberation movement, Mandela claimed, "Religion was one of the motivating factors in everything we did" (speech delivered to the Parliament of the World's Religions, December 5, 1999).

[4]I'm referring to television personality Oprah Winfrey and to Michael Caine's characterization of the butler "Alfred" in *The Dark Knight* (2008) and *Batman Begins* (2005). But I'm also invoking the National Study of Youth and Religion's description of the dominant God-images among American teenagers: Most view God as either a divine therapist whose primary function is to help you feel better, or a cosmic butler who comes when called but otherwise stays out of the way. See Christian Smith and Melinda Lundquist Denton, *Soul Searching: The Religious and Spiritual Lives of American Teenagers* (New York: Oxford University Press, 2004).

[5]Don't miss the endnotes of this book; they make an illuminating essay all by themselves.

Jenna, an 8th-grade girl, sat on a stool in front of 30 of her youth group peers one night during a winter retreat. The room they were in was rustic—wood mixed with dust—at a camp. Everyone was silent, watching Jenna. She squirmed, trying to remember the answer. But she took too long.

I pushed a button connected via wires to a contraption affixed underneath the seat of Jenna's stool, which was also connected to a wire screen wrapped over the top of the seat. Instantly, an electrical charge zapped Jenna, sending what felt like a million needles into her hind end. She screamed and lunged from the stool, much to the delight of the rest of the group who broke into cheers.

Jenna couldn't remember the Bible verse fast enough. So I shocked her on "the hot seat."

I agree we *need* to change. But the larger question remains: Are we willing to change? Or do we remain the child who believes that because he cannot see anyone from the inside of the blanket that no one will notice him from the outside? —*Andrew Seely*

Sadly youth ministry has become an entertainment venture for most churches. Youth pastors feel pressure to just get kids in the door—and if possible, get them saved. Encouraging them to become like Jesus isn't the goal; numbers are the goal. Since youth pastors also believe they must try to hang on to the students they have, they've moved to what I call a "raw" youth ministry—where we appeal to students' raw human nature that's so prevalent within modern media.
—*James C*

Why have we moved on? Perhaps it's because we're rediscovering the power (and necessity) of life-affirming relationships in youth ministry. And relationships are organic—they can't be facilitated by a hot seat or any other gimmick.
—*Jake Bouma*

Seriously. The hot seat was the laugh-riot, everyone-begged-for-it centerpiece of our winter retreat each year in the early '80s.

If I had a hot seat in my youth ministry today, I'd likely get sued. Or, at the very least, incur the significant wrath of some parents and lose my job. But things were different then. Right?

It's quite easy for me to look back at the hot seat now and think, *Wow. Why did we think that was okay?* It's a little embarrassing, to say the least—especially the fact that I used it to encourage Scripture memory!

But it raises a few questions to ponder:

• Was the hot seat *ever* okay?
• Has it gone by the wayside *only* because our culture has become so litigious?
• If it *was* okay, then why isn't it okay now?
• If it *wasn't* okay, then why didn't we realize that back then?

These questions aren't as simple as they might seem. If hot seats were semi-common in youth ministry in the '70s and on

I believe the youth ministry experiment has failed. We've made youth ministry glorified, professionalized—and hopefully in the future it will be dismantled and reevaluated. —*Gman*

I lost my job as a youth pastor in the mid-'90s over a mooning incident. In hindsight I can see how stupid and irresponsible my actions were, but this is what had been modeled to me by youth leaders when I was a teen in the 1980s. Despite all the idiotic and misguided things that happened in youth ministry in the '80s, I still found Christ in the relationships that I established there. But it's a different day. We need to see our calling as shepherds and priests and learn how to help fill the longing in adolescents' hearts for identity, belonging, and significance through deep, loving relationships and pointing them to Jesus. —*Howie*

The hot seat reminds me of a saying I adopted a while ago about ministry: "Everything has an expiration date." —*Jess R*

through the mid-'80s, and if the students all thought it was fun, and if no parents complained, and if youth ministry books suggested using them, then was it really wrong? In other words, if the common understanding among youth workers and the encouragement from the youth ministry collective was "hot seats are good," then does that make them good?

Or maybe you're thinking, *No, hot seats were morally wrong. The youth workers of that era just didn't see it.*

But why didn't we see it? Why wasn't there a backlash—from anyone?

These are the kinds of questions I'd like to take a stab at in this little book. But instead of looking at silly, micro issues such as hot seats, I intend to focus on the broader, macro questions surrounding our assumptions about youth ministry today.

I believe we're at a crossroads in youth work. In order to be effective—in order to be true to our calling—we need to

I'm not a youth worker but wanted to share this, as I was one of those youths who "fell through the cracks."

During a couple of summers in the early '90s, my parents shipped me away to Christian summer camp. I was around 13 years old. Both summers I left the camp completely uninterested, uninspired, and untouched. Why? Besides not feeling as though the group represented me, I never felt acknowledged on a personal level by any of the youth leaders. They always assumed we'd meet them at their level through the different activities and sessions they'd planned. But they didn't realize it had to be about meeting us at our level. They always seemed to focus on the "group" rather than us as individuals.

With increasing violence and substance abuse and more disadvantaged, broken homes than ever before, kids are just dying to be acknowledged. They need somebody to connect with them on a personal level. They need leaders who'll take the time to listen and affirm that they're okay, and they're loved—no matter who they are, where they're from, or what they're dealing with. If that connection isn't made, it's highly unlikely that youth will allow leaders to take them on something so sacred as a spiritual journey.
—*michball*

What in today's context are the vehicles to develop relationships with students that can truly impact their spiritual development? What aspects of youth culture do we infiltrate in order to do so? Is it through technology or social networks, sports, or music? The Christian faith has been about relationships since the days of the Gospels. Whether in youth ministry or church at large, as we seek to reinvent the future, we must be cautious that in reacting to what we correctly identify as problems, we don't let the pendulum swing back to the stiff, disconnected, and often legalistic environment that spawned many of the churches we were raised in. —*Mike*

change. We need to turn at this crossroad. But I'm afraid we're passing right through it, assuming the way we've always done things will continue to work.

The problem is this: The way we're doing things is *already not working*. We're failing at our calling. And deep down, most of us know it. This is why we need an epochal shift in our assumptions, approaches, models, and methods.

It's time for Youth Ministry 3.0.

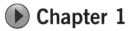

Chapter 1

THE NEED FOR CHANGE

Have you ever had a vision for a perfect day of adventure and found that the reality didn't even come close? I experienced this in an acute manner in Mendoza, Argentina, in the fall of 2006.

I was in Mendoza for one of Youth Specialties' Spanish youth worker conventions (called the *Convención Internacional Liderazgo Juvenil*). On the Sunday afternoon of the event, I had a bunch of free time. So two friends and I decided to find an adventure. We talked to a woman working at a tourist kiosk about getting tickets for a car race happening just outside of town. But she informed us the event was sold out and suggested we take a winery tour on bicycles.

Mendoza is the Napa Valley of Argentina, and it's peppered with hundreds of wineries. Though a winery tour on bikes sounded a bit too *Mary Poppins*-ish for us guys, we didn't have a lot of other options. And we thought it might be just weird enough to create some fun moments and memories.

The woman gave us instructions, maps, and bus passes; and off we went, confident in our expectation of a perfect day.

After riding a municipal bus for about 45 minutes—and constantly wondering if we'd missed it—we finally reached our stop. Hopping off, we found ourselves in a dusty, industrial estate on the edge of town. It was completely non-scenic and non-touristy, but we were headed toward another tourist ki-osk—one with the bikes.

Except it was closed.

At this point we had our first angel encounter of the day: An older, heavyset Argentine woman carrying way too many grocery bags walked up and engaged us in a sort of mime/charades con-versation. (We didn't speak Spanish; she didn't speak English.)

She mimed, "Are you fine-looking gentlemen trying to find bicycles to rent?"

We expertly mimed our response, "Yes!"

The angelic woman pointed down the road to a cheery ban-ner and said, "*Bicicletas.*" Even with my D in high school Span-ish, I knew enough to understand that one.

With renewed vigor, we set off in the direction of this pri-vate bike-rental facility. As it turned out, it was really a cin-derblock enclosure containing a rabid dog on a chain, a small house, and six bikes in the kitchen. But we paid our money and got our bikes before heading out with (once again) revitalized excitement for what lay ahead.

I can honestly say that for the first 100 or 200 yards, I was thinking to myself, *This is fantastic! What a weird and won-derful thing to do! We're going to have a blast!*

But shortly thereafter I started to feel the first twinges of pain. I saw that my back tire was low on air. I noticed there was a horrible headwind blowing against any forward prog-ress. And now I could feel my heart racing and my leg muscles getting all noodly.

After about a mile, I told my friends I had to stop and rest for a bit. After another half mile, we stopped a second time. The third stop was a quarter mile later. And the fourth was a few hundred feet past the third stop.

Two things occurred at this point:

First, I started to seriously consider whether or not I would die—that day—while on the side of the road in rural Argentina.

Second, one of my "friends" whipped out his camera phone and shot a mean little video of me panting, gasping, and clutching my chest. (Thankfully, since this is a book, I have no way of showing it to you.[1])

I had to concede; I had to go back. So we rode back to the "rental facility" only to find the front gate closed and no one home. Jimmying open the gate, we were soon met by the now-unchained rabid dog. We quickly discovered that throwing our bikes at the dog slowed him down just long enough for us to get back outside the gate and close it behind us. Rabies narrowly avoided.

I'll condense this next part: We walked, hopped on various buses, sat on rocks and logs, tried to hitchhike—and all in the general direction we thought we were supposed to go. Eventually, we were completely lost and making up imaginary headlines: "Stupid Gringos Disappear Outside Mendoza; Authorities Wonder Why They Were Riding Bikes."

Then it appeared. (Insert angel choir sound here.) Walking along a small tree-lined lane, we came across what could best be described as a rural Argentine 7-Eleven. And—get this—it was called "Emmanuel," which, of course, means "God with us."

We decided this God-with-us store would be our winery tour today. Exhausted, we purchased beverages and sat at a picnic table out front, laughing at our misfortune and stupidity. Three semi-toothless guys at the next table laughed at and with us.

So we started the mime game with them, somehow explaining where we'd been trying to go. They explained the winery was just around the corner, and we begged them to shuttle us there on their little moped. Explaining why this was not possible, they pointed to me, pretended to sit on an imaginary moped, then squatted low, indicating that my "size" would bring doom to their transportation.

Eventually, we convinced them to take the other guys on the moped (I had to walk), and we got to the winery...just as it was closing.

Our Efforts Aren't Meeting Our Expectations

For most of us who've been doing youth ministry for a while (and some who haven't been doing youth ministry for a while), I believe there's a sense of this story: The reality that's playing out is somewhat different than what we imagined, hoped, or expected.

> We, as the church, somehow, some way, need to develop an authentic community so individuals hunger for it and realize that nothing else will feed that hunger.
> —Jeff Greathouse

> The difficulty with changing and evolving our methods is that it often takes two to three years before we'll know for sure if our shift was a great new direction or a wrong turn. Mutations, morphs, and evolution involve lots of little changes over time, and sadly most youth workers don't have the patience for that. —Lukefish

While there's wonderful stuff happening in youth ministry all over the place—in pretty much every youth ministry—our impact, the transformation of kids' lives, seems less than we'd hoped. Study after study is bringing this harsh reality into focus. Kids are dropping out of church after youth group at staggering rates[2] (as high as 50 to 70 percent in one reputable survey[3]). And those students *in* our youth groups seem to be—according to researchers—subscribing to a faith that's neutered and unsustainable.[4]

To be fair, we youth workers are doing what we've always done—trying to love teenagers to the best of our abilities and help them experience the love of God. Our hearts are right (for the most part), but—I believe—there are flaws in many of our assumptions and methods. A disconnect.

Some of these flaws exist because we wrongly adopted cultural priorities into our youth ministry thinking. But more often our flaws exist because while our thinking was correct—for its time—the world of teenagers has changed, and we've been slow in our response.

It's like this: When you're in a poor, rural country and see a horse-drawn wagon rolling down a dirt road, you think nothing of it. It fits. But when you're driving through Pennsylvania Dutch country and see a horse-drawn buggy rolling down a nice, paved road and holding up traffic, it seems as though something doesn't fit. In many ways youth ministry today is the latter horse-drawn buggy.

Kenda Creasy Dean, in *Practicing Passion*, indicates that what teens are looking for is a faith worth dying for—something so important that it's worth giving one's life to completely. As far as I've seen it, our current models of ministry are largely failing to present faith in such a light. Instead it's a fun place to be with your friends—come for the food, stay for the Bible.

And maybe this is a greater symptom of, not youth ministry, but the family. If parents and mentors outside of youth ministry have the greatest impact on students' faith, this makes me think that youth ministry is just spinning its wheels—trying the wrong cure for the disease. Maybe what Youth Ministry 3.0 means is focusing on the family as a collection of interdependent people, not simply focusing on teens as individuals without regard to other influences in their lives. If nothing else, this means it's misguided to think that the "drop-out rate" is solely the fault of youth ministry. Maybe the greater fault is the failure to parent our children well. —*dan*

For all the talk of change and "if only we..." I find that often the best answers are the same as in the past: Not the extreme-game aspect...or the truth chair...but the idea of incarnational living among students. I cannot see that ever changing. —*Brandon*

Our Past, Present, and Future

Some time ago, a consultant working with our leadership team at Youth Specialties introduced us to a timeline exercise. (Interestingly, he's also one of the "friends" who was with me on that horrible day in Argentina.) He placed three pieces of paper on the floor; on each piece a word was printed, creating a physical timeline: PAST, PRESENT, and FUTURE. We each took turns standing on the pieces of paper, moving between them, and thinking about our lives, and where we're headed.

Recently I worked with the board of a nonprofit organization struggling with its identity. I used this same timeline exercise, but I had board members step into past, present, and future as an embodiment of the organization. I'd like to take a pass at that with this book: Looking back at our past, looking at our present, and attempting to describe a preferred future.

I'm not looking into a crystal ball—and this isn't an exercise in *predicting* the future. Instead, I'm hoping to describe what I'm seeing and experiencing and feeling about where we need to go so we can continue being true to our calling.

Running into a Hole in the Ground

As I write this, there's a series of Wendy's TV commercials that show ordinary people—often guys—wearing red braids and having countercultural epiphanies about burgers and other fast-food realities. My favorite of these commercials opens with an aerial shot of a massive hole in the ground, and hundreds of people are running toward it from all sides. When they get to the hole, they all jump in.

Then the shot changes to catch the face of one guy (wearing the red Wendy's wig) who's running amid the crowd. As he's running, we can hear his thoughts as he realizes that something isn't right. He then starts to speak as it dawns on him that he doesn't have to have his burgers cooked ahead of time and kept warm under a heat lamp. He slows to a stop, and a few others also stop to listen—but while most of the crowd continues to run into the hole. The few who stop with him all decide that they want their burgers to sizzle! They cheer and start running back—against the flow of the crowd.[5]

It's a funny commercial. But I have to admit that every time I see it, it reminds me of the church in North America. We have all this momentum. We perceive things are going well. Our megachurches are more mega than ever. Our youth ministries are better funded than ever. Youth ministry is receiving more respect than ever. We have better resources and training events and celebrities and credibility than we've ever had.

So why does it seem like we're racing into a hole?

I want to be part of that countercultural band of youth workers who stop. I want to be part of that "wait a second" group that doesn't accept the way things are. I want to join with others who notice that we're heading down a path toward obsolescence and complete ineffectiveness and turn around to ask, "What should we change?"

Chapter 2

FRAMING CHANGE IN YOUTH CULTURE

Adolescence, as you likely know, is a fairly recent cultural phenomenon. Wait. Let me be Captain Obvious and take a step backward: Adolescence is a cultural phenomenon (recent or not).

Sure, there are loads of physiological markers, transitions, and unique elements in regard to adolescence. We can talk about (or, more accurately, I could write about) cognitive development and emotional changes and relational groupings and moral and spiritual shifts for a long time. I could even write a long chapter or two about the exciting new developments in adolescent brain research and some of the potential implications for youth ministry. These excursions are tempting, as both are passions of mine, and it would be a great way to bulk up the number of these pages until they reach "real book" size. But I'll resist; it's not my point. That said, adolescence clearly has biological, developmental, and physiological markers and boundaries.

But adolescence has been, and still is, a *cultural phenomenon.*

Let's face it: Girls, from the first daughter of Eve, have had first periods (menarche)—one of the physiological markers of the onset of puberty in females. (Actually, developing breast buds and pubic hair are the earliest indicators of puberty onset in girls.) But there was no adolescence—at least not a culturally acknowledged period of time—until about 100 years ago.[6] There

So if adolescence is a cultural phenomenon (to an extent), isn't it entirely possible that we're embarking on a new cultural development, where everyone becomes adolescent-like? (We could call it *post-adolescence* if we wanted to sell books.) Perhaps this rapid culture change will demand new terms as we frame change in youth ministry...perhaps even the terms *youth ministry, youth group*, and *youth pastor* need to be phased out. —*James*

was "youth," but not adolescence. Youth was merely another word for "child." And that made sense, given the context.

So what was it—more than 100 years ago—that caused G. Stanley Hall to use the term adolescence in his book by the same title?[7] Hall (and others) had observed a new culturally accepted "holding period"—a pause button—between the carefree life of a child and the expectations of adulthood. This pause, which Hall called *adolescence*, was culture's way of providing teenagers with a respite to wrestle with a few issues.[8]

Hall talked of adolescence as a time of "Storm and Stress" (a hat tip to the German *Sturm und Drang* movement). Hall wrote that this developmental phase had three key elements that were common to all: Conflict with parents, mood disruptions, and risky behavior.[9]

Furthermore—and central to the notion of this book—over the next 50 years, Hall and others began talking about the tasks of adolescence in a three-fold manner that, while exact wording gets bantered about and tweaked by different people, hasn't really changed much.[10] I'll return to this in a moment.

The Growth of Youth Culture

The emergence of adolescence—and, particularly, the expansion of adolescence and the rise of youth culture—is the result of a symbiotic dance between physiology and culture. Here's what I mean: In 1904, when Granville Stanley Hall (Yo, G!) published *Adolescence*, the boundaries he describes, in a sense, still exist. In another sense, the boundaries have completely changed—and radically so.

Adolescence is the period between puberty and adulthood. More accurately, it's the period of life between puberty and a culture's expectation of adultlike engagement in culture at large—becoming a fully contributing member of society. That part hasn't changed.

What *has* changed, among other things, are the *actual* ages these descriptions represent. The funny thing is that the low-end age marker has changed due to physiology, and the upper-end age marker has changed due to cultural issues. And, of course, it's never quite that simple (as if the pubertal entry gate into adolescence didn't have any cultural input or implications).

When Hall described adolescence, he was talking about a period of time 18 months long. That's right: A year and a half. That's it! So it's no wonder there wasn't much of a "youth culture" back then. In the early 1900s, the average age for

It's sad that we "adults" are failing to usher in our children as adults. It's as if we (adults) don't know what we're doing yet to teach our youth what it means to be an adult. I believe, now more than ever, that we need to broaden our focus. Yes, teens are important... but so are their parents. So let's reach out to them; place mentors in their lives as well. Teach the parents how to parent in a way that raises their children to grow up and continue to surround our teens with adults who'll guide and usher them into the world and the body of faith as spiritually mature, independent, and contributing adults. —*Josh*

And how does this 15-year period of adolescence affect youth ministers? Many nowadays are under the age of 30, myself included. Am I an adolescent ministering to fellow adolescents? And who's discipling the adolescent youth pastors? Do we now need a youth pastor for the youth pastors? —*Joel*

It used to be that people got married and began having children at age 13 or so. (My grandmother, for example, was married at 13 and had her first child at 15). It's only been within the last 100 years that adolescence has expanded, and now we tell our teens they need to wait for marriage—plus, the culturally accepted time for marriage is getting later and later. However, biologically, teens are still in the same place that their grandparents and great-grandparents were; in fact, they're reaching puberty at an earlier age.

I've often wondered if that's part of the reason why teens are so rebellious. Biologically they are "adults"—and even just 100 years ago would have been treated as such. Now our society is trying to keep them from reaching that stage more and more: How many of us know 25- to 27-year-olds still living at home with parents?

We need to find a way to bring the two together—to help the kids deal with what's going on biologically, yet still within the accepted societal norms...or we change the norms. It was just over 100 years ago that daily bathing became common, thanks to Queen Victoria—now we can't imagine any other way. So why can't we change the norms surrounding adolescence? —*Miranda*

the onset of puberty in girls was 14.5.[11] And Hall suggested that our shifting culture was allowing an 18-month window of time—until about the age of 16—to wrestle with the adolescent tasks of identity, autonomy, and affinity.

Fast-forward to the 1970s: The entry point to adolescence (the biological marker of puberty) for girls had dropped to an average of 13 years old, and the exit point (of course, it's not a hard-and-fast exit point) had seen a cultural shift to 18 years old. Now teenagers had an average of six years to wrestle with these adolescent issues. Additionally—and this is important—this greater quantity of years also meant that the number of teenagers engaged in this process was a massively higher percentage of the culture at large (due not only to population growth, but also to the span of the demographic). Therefore, teenagers had significantly more sway over culture at large.[12]

Fast-forward again to the turn of the millennium. The average age for the onset of puberty in girls is now 10.5 to 11 years old.[13,14] And the culturally accepted norm for when an adolescent is expected to function as a contributing member of society (and to have made significant progress in the three tasks of adolescence)? The number is fuzzier than ever, but most agree it's somewhere in the mid- to upper-20s.

So—hold onto your youth pastor job descriptions—adolescence is now *15 or more years long.* This reality is both *impacted* by culture and has a massive *impact on* culture.[15]

What I find most interesting is that if adolescence isn't finding its closure until the mid- to late-twenties, then what does that say for youth workers? I'm 22 and have been in the field for three years now. Back in early 1900, I would've been an adult; today I'm lumped in with the "young adults" (which is a nice way of saying I'm still a kid). So should we hire youth workers who are 30 and older? Most people seem to think that's when you begin losing your "edge" in youth ministry; but developmentally, that's when you're just beginning to have the "edge" you need—being at the point we want our students to reach. So which do we want in youth workers? Adolescents leading adolescents—or bona-fide adults leading adolescents? —*Kyle*

The Three Tasks of Adolescence

All teenagers, at least those who live in a culture that acknowledges adolescence, wrestle with identity, autonomy, and affinity—Hall's three "tasks of adolescence." I refer to them as tasks, though they're almost completely wrestled with semiconsciously. The older teenagers get, the more self-aware they become of this wrestling, of these tasks (and certainly more so these days since adolescence now stretches into the 20s). But the tasks present themselves at the onset of adolescence.

Identity

Dictionaries define identity as:

Condition or character as to who a person or what a thing is.[16]

This is what's needed: A church for young people that will know how to speak to their hearts and enkindle, comfort, and inspire enthusiasm in them with the joy of the gospel and the strength of the Eucharist; a church that will know how to invite and welcome the person who seeks a purpose for which to commit his whole existence; a church that's not afraid to require much, after having given much; that does not fear asking from young people the effort of a noble and authentic adventure, such as that of the following of the gospel (adapted from John Paul II, 1995 World Day of Prayer for Vocations). —*D. Scott Miller*

The distinct personality of an individual regarded as a persisting entity; individuality.[17] *Who a person is, or the qualities of a person or group which make them different from others.*[18]

For our purposes, we'll define *identity* as the "Who am I?" question. Simply put: One's identity is the sum of one's self-perceptions. This includes self-perceptions about character, values, purpose, and potential in life; caste; emotional makeup; appearance and body type; intellectual, spiritual, and emotional strength or weakness; relationship to family and friends and culture at large; and many other factors.[19]

Children and preteens aren't intellectually capable of this kind of third-person thought. A nine-year-old cannot stand apart from herself and perceive herself, cannot form opinions of herself based on self-perception. She can form opinions about herself based only on what she likes or doesn't like and what others have said about her.

The kind of thinking required for identity formation is truly brand-spanking new in adolescence, and it's a direct result of the gift of abstract thinking.[20] Abstract thinking goes beyond concrete, tangible, linear, and black-and-white. In short, it could be characterized as *thinking about thinking.*

The addition of abstract thinking brings the teenager a whole host of new abilities, such as:

- **Hypothesizing.** Abstract thinking allows teenagers (and adults, of course) to create multiple scenarios—real or imaginary—of "what might be." Teenagers are just beginning to consider likely, and unlikely, down-the-line results of various actions and choices —both their own actions and choices, and the actions and choices of others. Of course, they're also really bad at this because it's a new ability. But they have the basic cognitive tools to do it.[21]

Of the three tasks of adolescence, it seems as though the church really only tries to help with autonomy by emphasizing that students make their faith their own. While youth ministry focuses some on identity, it seems to be more of a mainstreaming approach that strips away freedom and forces students into the narrow confines in which the church traditionally sees Christian-guy-and-girl roles. As for affinity, youth ministries seem to desire one affinity group for students at the expense of all the other groups. This leads to an all-or-nothing mentality, the ostracization of "fringe" kids, and the glorification of the dedicated.
—*josh mcalister*

- **Speculating.** Closely linked to hypothesizing, speculation is directly tied to decision-making and is the practice of thinking through likely outcomes. We adults do this quickly (most of the time) and intuitively. When presented with a choice, we immediately (again, in most cases) speculate about the likely outcomes of the various options. We might call this "making an informed decision." Again, children and preteens aren't capable of making an informed decision as they don't possess the ability to speculate.

• **Empathizing.** I live near Tijuana, Mexico, which is filled with poverty. If I take my two children to visit families living in a Tijuana garbage dump, scavenging for food and sustenance, then my children will likely have two very different experiences. Max, my 10-year-old—a naturally sensitive boy—will experience deep sympathy regarding the plight of the children and families he encounters. He'll feel bad for them and want to help. Liesl, my 14-year-old daughter, however, will likely experience empathy. She'll also feel bad for the children she sees, but she'll take it a step further. She'll empathize as she imagines (even "feels") what life would be like for an impoverished child. She'll "place herself in that child's shoes" and perceive life from that perspective, a perspective completely third person and outside of herself. She might also wrestle with abstract questions, such as, "Why was this child born in this place and to this poverty? And why was I born to the comfortable life that I have?"

• **Doubting.** Doubting, of course, occurs when we internally question our beliefs. This is a very abstract thought process, and it's not possible prior to adolescence. But it's absolutely essential to faith development and a wonderful developmental gift in God's design.

• **Emoting.** Emotions are abstract! And since children don't think abstractly, they're significantly limited in their emotional options. I like to think of this as if children are going through life with an emotional "painter's palette" that contains a limited number of colors (emotional options): Just the primary colors and a few simple secondary combinations. But with the onset of puberty and the gift of abstract thinking, that small palette is replaced by a massive new emotional palette with hundreds of nuanced and complex emotions, as well as a massive glob of black to add dimension, broodiness, and all other things emotionally dark!

• **Self-perceiving.** I've already mentioned this, but preteens don't have the ability to think of themselves beyond what they see in the mirror or what others say about them. But abstract thinking brings the ability to think about oneself and to speculatively perceive oneself from another's perspective. Once again, teenagers—especially younger ones—are notoriously bad at this. They often incorrectly perceive how others see them and assume everyone is "checking them out."[22]

• And, of course, **identity formation.**

It would be wrong to say that identity formation *begins* in adolescence. Our identities are being formed from day one. All the messages we absorb from family, friends, and the culture at large form who we perceive ourselves to be. The shift that occurs in adolescence—thanks to our friend, abstract thinking—is that teenagers suddenly acquire the ability to take charge of their own identity formation. Since they gain self-perception (and all the other implications just discussed), they can begin directing the course of their identity formation. They make choices and see the implications of who they are and who they're becoming. They begin to speculate about who they

Adolescents are trying everything in their power to figure out who they are by asking three questions: 1. *Where in the world do I fit?* 2. *Who am I?* 3. *Do I matter?* What if a few adults came alongside them to affirm their adolescent process? How cool would it be for adults to assist in the adolescent journey?

We youth workers so often tell adolescents what we think they should become. Rather we should be affirming what they're becoming. —*jeremy z*

I recall hearing a speaker say that a generation ago, people tended to first find Jesus then find a church to belong to. Now the trend is to first search for belonging within the church, then—once belonging is found—they find Jesus. I'm extrapolating from this that youth are also looking for somewhere to belong. It may be a church; it may be a gang.

We need to provide a positive, safe, nurturing place where Jesus is offered in a loving and patient way. We need to glorify Jesus but not beat kids kids up with him. I see this desire for belonging as the affinity you're describing.
—*Dave*

want to be, not only in regard to what careers they'd like to have someday, but also in regard to what kind of people they want to be and what kind of people they want others to identify them as. In other words, adolescence provides the opportunity to choose who one becomes.

This is why identity is such a major task in adolescence. The reality is that by the time an adolescent reaches her mid-20s, her identity will be mostly formed. (And, remember, this is the whole point of culture giving teenagers a respite between childhood and adulthood.) Sure, we all continue to shape and refine our identities throughout adulthood, but the core formation work is done. The course is mostly set.

Autonomy

The word *autonomy* simply refers to something's separateness—its independence. In adolescent-development terms, autonomy is wrestling with the questions "How am I unique and different?" and "What's my unique contribution?"

I asked Dr. Chap Clark for help in defining *autonomy*, and

he gave me this extremely helpful response: "The essence of the development of autonomy is the acquisition and application of personal power, or more technically, *agency*. That means that not only are kids on the trek to discover who they are, but they also need to ultimately believe that they matter, that they're agents with power, and that the world needs them."[23]

You can easily see how this is directly and completely tied to the growth in abstract thinking we just talked about. Children may see themselves as unique in some way(s). But cognitive development and abstract thinking allows the addition of comparison and third-person perception. Children will define themselves primarily *in relation* to others—usually family. But teenagers begin to define themselves *in opposition* to others (often *especially* their families!). Teenagers are constantly drawing conclusions (correct or incorrect) about others and defining themselves *against* those. "I'm not like him (or her or them)" becomes important to the task of autonomy.

In psychological terms, this is often referred to as *individuation*. The process of individuation is becoming oneself, unique,

> The constant tension of youth ministry seems to be the previous generation of teenagers—i.e., the ones who thrived on autonomy. And they can't understand why we'd attempt to stress something different. It almost seems as though the autonomy they desired has followed into their homes, and now their children are asking, "If everyone is just an individual at home, where can I belong?"
> —*Jake*

> It seems as though running a youth ministry should always be based on, "Who are these kids?" and "What are their stories?" That seems like the starting point when trying to successfully work within the tasks of identity, autonomy, and affinity—because ultimately theirs are the stories that need to be told…not ours. But I've got no other methodology for that apart from experimentation and instinctive responsiveness. Is there a better way? —*tash*

and separate. This process is primarily (though not exclusively) the issue of separating from one's family.

Mixed into this progression is the ancillary question "What's my unique contribution?"[24] This is a swirling, cyclical dance partner with the "How am I unique?" question, as the two constantly inform each other and help each other to progress. The "contribution" in that question plays out in a variety of arenas: Family, friends, and other relationships; school; youth group; community; and the world. As a teenager begins to see her uniqueness, she's better equipped to understand her role and influence in relationships and the world around her. And as she begins to see how that influence in relationships and the world around her plays out, she's better equipped to grasp her uniqueness.

Affinity

Affinity, as a word, simply means likeness or attraction. We use it in a developmental sense to refer to people's connections to others who are like them in some way. This "likeness" may be external—a teenage boy may find affinity with guys who are into skateboarding

> Marko, does a focus on affinity cause an unnecessary focus on self? I think of all these verses that tell us to die to self, to decrease (so Jesus can increase), to look to others' interests rather than our own, etc., and then I wonder how that fits into your idea of affinity.
> —*Curtis McGill*

> Curtis, I think you're making a false assumption that affinity is a selfish task (or, somehow more selfish than the other two—really, they're all about self, which is a natural, God-designed part of adolescent development). Affinity is about finding where and to whom one belongs. —*Marko*

> Marko, I agree that they need to find out who and where they belong. Should it be the key transition point? I don't agree that our focus on self is God-designed. It's a result of the fall. It's a part of humanity that we need to work with and understand, though. Maybe we spend too much time chasing an ever-changing culture.
> —*Curtis McGill*

or science, or a teenage girl may find affinity with the group of kids who like a certain style of music. But the likeness can also be more internal. A teenager can find affinity with others who share the same values or the same outlook on life. Or a teenager can find affinity with his family based on shared experiences and story.

This final task of adolescence almost seems in opposition to the task of autonomy. But, in reality, they go hand in hand—two apparent opposites in a dependent dance, with identity looking on. Autonomy and affinity are the yin and yang of identity formation, really, informing and framing that first task.

It's easy to see this quest for affinity in teenagers. They desperately desire to be included, to be part of a social network, to feel as though they belong somewhere. Young and middle teens, especially, commonly have multiple affinity groups to which they belong (or aspire to belong). This is all a normal (sometimes healthy, sometimes not) part of the process of figuring out who they are.

Affinity is a crucial step in adolescent development. But how will the church respond? Will we entrust the youth pastor with the responsibility of being the only shepherd for our youth? Or will the youth pastor share that responsibility with the congregation? It's great to give youth a "safe" place to belong in our youth ministries... but if we haven't given them a place to belong after they graduate from high school (lets not forget extended adolescence!), then we've failed miserably. It's crucial that adults and families reach out to youth and make them part of their lives. —Ben

I can't help but think our model for practicing the art of presence is right in the Emmaus story in Luke 24:13-35—in that when we stop and listen, we actually begin to see God be God and recognize that God works even in the midst of the journey Christ calls us to walk. —KC

As I write this, my wife and I are becoming increasingly aware of this process in our 14-year-old daughter's life. Liesl

Where I see the breakdown with youth (and many adults) is the thinking that certain affinity groups are godless. For whatever reason—be it culture, group dynamics, selfishness, or fear—certain affinity groups are viewed as void of God. For some reason we now expect, allow, and have grown comfortable with this line of thinking. For example, "God is at camp but not at school," or "God is at youth group but not the movie theater," or "God is near when I'm with my family, but not when I'm with my friends."

What I've been trying to affirm and encourage with my teens is the reality that in every situation/group they find themselves, God is present and active.

Your last paragraph about Liesl being "three different girls" really hits home. I've been harping on my kids to be the same person in each group. Perhaps this is misguided. Regardless, it seems to me that when a kid's identity and autonomy are under construction, we as youth workers need to make every effort to help our students understand that even though their affinity groups have different identities, Christ hopes to be situated at the center of their lives. —*Tom*

finds affinity with her church friends (and particularly with her middle school small group from church). She finds affinity with a particular group of friends at school. And she finds affinity with our family. We're discovering how she's three different girls, in many ways, within these three settings: Guarded yet engaged in the first, bubbly and crass in the second, and loving but aloof at home. If she were an adult, we'd probably say she's being disingenuous in at least one, if not two, of those settings and that only one of them brings out her true self. But for an adolescent, Liesl is all three of those girls, living into—*as well* as leveraging against—all three in order to define herself.[25]

A Proposal for Framing Change

I have a proposal upon which the rest of this book rests. I believe proof for it is evident in youth culture, visible for anyone who keenly observes the changing lives of adolescents in general.

My proposal is this: While these three adolescent tasks (identity, autonomy, and affinity) have continued to be the defining mud-wrestling pit of the adolescent experience, *the prioritization of the three has shifted through the various eras of modern youth culture.*

Summary
The three tasks of adolescence are:

- Identity—"Who am I?"

- Autonomy—"How am I unique and different?" and "What's my unique contribution?"

- Affinity—"Where do I belong and to whom?"

In the earliest days of modern youth culture (post–World War II through the 1960s), *identity* was at the top of the priority list for adolescence in general.

Once youth culture was widely accepted and played a more significant role in Western culture at large (1970s through the end of the 20th century), *autonomy* was upgraded to the top priority spot.

And now in this post-millennial era in which we find ourselves, the dominance of youth culture (a shift in which youth culture became the dominant culture of our world) has moved *affinity* to the top.

I'll unpack this notion further in the next chapter, but I'll tease this point now: *This is where youth ministry is failing.* We adjusted to the first change in priorities (from *identity* to *autonomy*), but we've been slow in our response to the second change (from *autonomy* to *affinity*). Youth ministries are built on assumptions and values and methods that are outdated for the teenagers we passionately want to serve today.

Chapter 3

YOUTH MINISTRY 1.0
POST-WORLD WAR II
THROUGH THE 1960S

I want to look back at an extremely brief history of the modern youth ministry movement.[26] But it's critical to remember that—as easy as it is to critique from our perspective—these youth workers were revolutionaries. They were trying to be true to their calling to connect teenagers to Jesus in the context of the culture of their time.

Youth Ministry 1.0

While adolescence was identified in the early 1900s, a wide variety of "youth movements" had already come and gone in North America, the UK, and Continental Europe since the mid-1800s.[27] "Youth culture"—as an established and widely acknowledged subculture—didn't really exist until after World War II, when postwar disillusionment combined with the financial stability of the '50s gave rise to a subculture defined on the surface by music, clothes, cars, and movie stars. But under the surface, this new subculture was more about freedom, attitude, spending power (a variable that often formalizes and calcifies a cultural subgroup, as marketing and product money are typically focused at that particular group, thus creating the cyclical effect of legitimizing it into a more powerful spending group), and...identity.[28]

Christian youth workers began springing up, sensing a radical, missional calling to reach teenagers for Jesus. This really was missionary work: Early youth workers saw themselves (rightly so) as bridging into a foreign culture with its own language, values, and codes of conduct. It's helpful to note that these earliest youth workers didn't try to become teenagers (or dress or act like teenagers), just as a good foreign missionary understands that she's a visitor.

Here's the odd thing about our youth ministry nexus (I use "our" as a youth worker who owns this as the history of my tribe): Churches, in general, were slow to respond to the rise of youth culture (big shock). Churches and church leaders equated youth culture with sinful activities or—at least—unwholesome activities and rebellious attitudes. So those early youth ministry pioneers who knew they had to be true to their calling found—in large measure—that they had to do youth ministry outside the context of the local church.

Enter the rise of Youth for Christ,[29] Young Life,[30] and a host of other parachurch organizations and youth evangelists. Remember, this wasn't the YFC and Young Life of today (or even the last 25 years) with campus clubs and relational youth workers. These were (mostly) white men wearing suits and preaching—using the culturally normative communication of the day—to rooms full of teenagers. Picture a rally, an evangelistic crusade, or a youth Sunday school class in which men in suits preach to eager audiences of teenagers while addressing the real issues of the youth world.

Christian teenagers, especially—and teenagers in general—were responsive to this missionary effort because they were completely unaccustomed to hearing adults, other than musicians and movie stars, speak to them in their language, about their issues, and in a way that wasn't exclusively pejorative and condescending.

Going back to my proposal that the three tasks of adolescence have reshuffled into a different prioritization in each of these eras, youth culture, at large, was **fixated on identity**. Not that autonomy and affinity weren't important—they surely were. But identity was the task *du jour*. Youth culture had that brand-new shininess to it, fresh out of the culture mill. It was still newly observed and largely undefined. It—if I can personify youth culture for a moment—didn't have a sense of itself yet and had only just become self-aware.

These early youth ministry missionaries rightly responded to youth culture by allowing it to inform the **language** and **topics** of youth ministry.

Of course, it's a generalization to say there were "key themes" of youth ministry in this era. And, to be fair, no one gathered up a group of the earliest youth workers and asked them to brainstorm and vote on key themes. But I'd suggest that the key themes in Youth Ministry 1.0 were **Evangelism** and **Correction**.

Evangelism

Early Christian youth workers saw themselves as missionaries to youth culture. And they saw their task, or calling, primarily in terms of bringing the gospel, in culturally understandable language and examples, to an unreached people group.[31] And reach them they did. These evangelistic efforts were highly successful. (And for many reasons, I'm sure, not the least of which would be the aforementioned hunger of teenagers to have adults speak to them in their own language, on their own terms.)

 47

> I disagree. We're still speaking of the evils of "youth culture" and parents still bring their kids to us in order that we may save them from the evils of youth culture (while at the same time advocating it in some degree in their own homes)—and as one of the greats of us said, "to make them nice." We're still doing youth ministry as if we don't understand that shift or task of adolescence. It is a seesaw between perception and reality. Perception: This is what reached me, therefore, it will reach those at the same age I was when I heard it. Reality: Even those of us in our early- to mid-20s are finding that the culture we came out of is drastically different. We would like it to be the same, but are faced with their reality. —*Jess*

Correction

But buried in these youth-appropriate messages was an underlying bias that youth culture was bad.[32] Youth culture, and the youth that populated it, needed correction, needed to turn away from the evils of youth culture (rebelliousness, idleness, carnality, licentiousness, wicked music, and a much longer list). Certainly, we continue to "preach" some of those messages today and for good reason. But we've also grown in our understanding of adolescent development and the adolescent experience, and we know that some of the things characterized as "evil" are merely the identity, autonomy, and affinity struggles of teenagers.

Interestingly, early youth workers were *not* preoccupied with how teenagers dressed or talked or the new freedoms they possessed. This was seen in a neutral "it is what it is" cultural reality.

For each of the three eras, I've wrestled with a "driver" for youth ministry, and the first two came to me quite easily. During Youth Ministry 1.0, youth ministry was primarily **proclamation-driven.** Small groups didn't really exist yet (not in the way we talk about or use them today). Creative curricula and games and mission trips, and all the rest of what has grown as an industry within the church, were not being used in large measure. Youth ministry was primarily about preaching to teenagers.

It's hardly fair to claim key themes for an era of youth culture; no one gathered together Billy Graham and his cronies to choose a theme verse for their attempts. But if I could claim one for them, with the benefit of hindsight, I'd choose Matthew 7:13-14—

Enter through the narrow gate. For wide is the gate
and broad is the road that leads to destruction, and
many enter through it. But small is the gate and narrow
the road that leads to life, and only a few find it.

	Youth Ministry 1.0	Youth Ministry 2.0	Youth Ministry 3.0
Youth Culture Fixation	Identity		
Cultural Influence on Youth Ministry	Language and Topics		
Key Themes	Evangelism and Correction		
Driver	Proclamation		
Theme Verse	Matthew 7:13-14		

We've seen the shift of youth ministry over the years to accommodate perceived needs in youth culture. After all, they once considered throwing out Sunday school at the turn of the 20th century when it failed to achieve its goal of the character development of students. I'm thankful that the shifting hasn't stopped, that we're active in our pursuit of Christ, and that we've continued diving into a culture that many of us left behind when it was much different.
—Jess

Then, in the late '60s and early '70s, some youth workers started thinking, *This isn't working. Something's wrong.* These second-wave youth workers ushered in what I'm calling Youth Ministry 2.0.

Parallels in Mainline Churches

Before we move on, I'd like to sidestep for a moment and acknowledge that much of what I've written here is a generalized and simplistic overview of *evangelical* youth ministry during this era. A parallel story was unfolding in mainline churches, and this spot between Youth Ministry 1.0 and 2.0 is a good place to mention it, as their story weaves into the next era.

As Youth Ministry 1.0 was taking shape and starting to get some very early traction in churches, there was a watershed year for mainline youth ministry—1965. In that year, the World Council of Churches (WCC) issued a statement encouraging churches to dismantle their youth ministries.[33] Their caution was actually rather insightful: They were concerned that youth ministries were becoming ghetto-ized and isolated (what an amazing foreshadowing of what was to come in Youth Ministry 2.0!) and insisted that youth should be integrated into the whole church.

Unfortunately, as my friend Dr. Kenda Dean (youth ministry professor at Princeton Theological Seminary) says, mainline denominations—almost across the board—took this as permission to cut youth ministry programs and budgets at the denominational level and not replace them with any intentional effort toward the integration part of the WCC's suggestion. According to Kenda, the subsequent decline in mainline church attendance, specifically in the early 1980s, led to further elimination of the remaining shards of youth ministry presence at denominational levels.[34]

In these transitional years (the early years of Youth Ministry 2.0), many youth workers with mainline affiliations found themselves growing up in, and sometimes working in, evangelical parachurch youth ministries. When they began entering church youth ministry (mainline churches still hired youth pastors left and right, like the evangelical church, during Youth Ministry 2.0), they brought with them what Andy Root calls "the personal, relational ministry toolbox" developed in evangelical parachurch ministries at the end of Youth Ministry 1.0 and the beginning of Youth Ministry 2.0.[35] These youth workers, with their mainline affiliations and theology, were greatly influenced by Youth Specialties and *Group Magazine*, as—pragmatists that youth workers tend to be—these were the only resources available at the time.

As a result, the parallel tracks of mainline and evangelical youth ministry came together in Youth Ministry 2.0.

Chapter 4

YOUTH MINISTRY 2.0
1970S THROUGH THE
END OF THE CENTURY

By the late 1960s, youth culture had come into its own. There was no more posing. (Think: Early '60s Beatles in suits with cropped, mop-top hair to late '60s Beatles in psychedelic hippie clothes with long hair.) Clearly a shift had taken place. Teenagers had no memory of a time when not everyone went to high school, no memory of a time when all children were expected to do whatever adults told them to do, no memory of a world without their own music and styles and values and celebrities. In the minds of a 1970s teenager, youth culture had always existed.

Churches were finally waking up to the need for youth ministry and moving beyond offering only a "young persons" Sunday school class. Youth groups sprang onto the church scene, and churches started hiring youth pastors left and right.[36] Parachurch youth ministry organizations began focusing more on kids outside of church, and churches began utilizing the methods forged by those parachurch youth workers in the safe and secure contexts of their church walls.

I am a child of this shift. The large church I attended in the Detroit area always had an active youth program. But it was while I was in junior high (in the early to mid-'70s) that our church hired its first youth pastor who was responsible only for

 53

high school students.[37] (We poor junior highers were still stuck in a nothing-but-Sunday-school system.)

Our youth group still attended the occasional Youth for Christ (or Voice of Christian Youth) rally, which was a holdover from Youth Ministry 1.0. But by the time I got to high school, these rallies had either ceased to exist, or we just stopped going to them. We didn't need them: We had a large, fully functioning youth group that met all of our programming needs (as well as our spiritual formation needs, I suppose). We were self-contained and active with a full assortment of retreats, camps, ski trips, bike trips, mission trips, midweek programming, Bible quizzing, teen choir, lock-ins, and everything else that a great youth ministry would dream of in the 1980s.

The Birth of Youth Specialties

The ministry I lead, Youth Specialties, was born at the beginning of this era. And the founders of Youth Specialties, Mike Yaconelli and Wayne Rice, played lead roles in this epochal shift. Both Mike and Wayne had been active participants in Youth Ministry 1.0 while working for Youth for Christ in the San Diego area. They'd cobbled together a friendship of sorts, based on a common calling and a common frustration with the church. But when they sensed the parachurch organization they loved calcify as churches were hiring youth pastors, both went on staff at local churches.

But just before Mike and Wayne left their parachurch roles, they'd developed some (then) revolutionary approaches to youth ministry that had less to do with preaching and more to do with creating community in a group of teenagers, interacting with them in real dialogue about real teen issues, helping them live out the gospel *within* their own culture (rather than encouraging them to come out of it), and deepening their understanding of adolescent development and how it should inform everything they did in youth ministry. Mike and Wayne had written down these "ideas" as the first Campus Life manual for Youth for Christ.

Now, I have a deep respect for YFC, and I'm very encouraged by their leadership today. But—and we've joked about this together—if it weren't for what happened next and the bullheadedness of YFC at the time, Youth Specialties wouldn't exist.

Mike and Wayne wanted to make their little collection of ideas available to other youth workers in churches, and they asked YFC for the stuff they'd written. When YFC denied their request, Mike and Wayne belligerently set out to completely rewrite it, making it better than before.

> Where are all those crazy youth workers from the '70s and '80s? They have a wealth of experience and wisdom to share with us—but what happened to them? Were they all pushed out by the politics of Kool-Aid-stained carpets? Do they sit around and have meetings discussing what could have been if someone would have just said "thanks"? Did ministry styles and programming issues pass them by? Were they just working their way to senior pastorates and saw youth ministry as a stepping stone? Where did they go? I don't have these answers. I wish I did. I also wish that these youth workers would come back and help us younger vets—and the rookies who are coming online beside us. The church could really use their abilities, giftings, and talents. I wish I knew how to talk them back into it! —*Scott Riley*

In 1969, Mike and Wayne hand made a hundred or so copies of this new book, which they (not so) creatively called *Ideas*. (The "Ideas Library" continues to be an important part of Youth Specialties' publishing effort to this day.) Mike typed up the copy and printed them out on a mimeograph machine at his church. Wayne silkscreened the covers on store-bought binders.

They took the books to an early gathering of youth workers at Forest Home Christian Conference Center (then Forest Home Camp) in the mountains outside of Los Angeles, and they literally sold them out of the trunk of their car—all of them.

That's when these two pioneers realized there was a huge need to resource church youth workers, and Youth Specialties was born.[38]

The Reification of Youth Culture and the Response of Teenagers

Let's jump back to youth culture at large for a moment. As we got used to the rising dominance of youth culture, entire industries sprang up to meet the demand of growing youth culture.[39] In short, youth culture became commoditized. And that commoditization both reinforced and reified the existence of this increasingly powerful subculture.

And a funny thing happened: The commoditization of youth culture, I would suggest, led to the confidence of youth culture. In a personified way, youth culture had the identity task fairly worked out. It knew who it was. And this was confirmed by both the marketers drooling for teenagers' dollars, as well as parents and churches and just about every other adult-run organization reacting *against* aspects of youth culture. For many adults, youth culture was like porn: Often outwardly derided, but secretly pursued. And this confirmed youth culture's understanding of itself.

This is when and why the prioritization of adolescent tasks shifted. With a clearer sense of identity, a sense of confidence, and an undisputed place in the consciousness of society, youth culture began a more earnest effort to define itself *in opposition*

to the culture at large. This is in the very DNA of youth culture, really—it will always work to become "other" and unique, always mutate to stay countercultural and rebellious.[40]

Of course, identity and affinity were still crucial tasks of adolescence, both for youth culture in general, and certainly for every individual teenager; but the top priority—the fixation—shifted to **autonomy**. This makes sense, doesn't it? If the whole nation is acknowledging youth culture, and many are even clamoring for it, then youth culture has to put a high priority on finding its uniqueness—and, in a positive way, finding its unique contribution—in order to maintain its newly formed, but still pliable, identity.

The Church Responds with Youth Ministry 2.0

This shift, I believe, is what the revolutionary youth workers of Youth Ministry 2.0 were responding to. With a passion to stay true to their calling to reach teenagers with the transformational gospel, a handful of youth workers began stepping into new forms of youth ministry to connect with teenagers in a changing culture. Relationships began to trump youth-y preaching, and youth groups sprang up—because, at the end of the day, what is a youth group other than a church within a church, a "youth church" semi-connected to the whole but distinctly other?

Concurrent with this youth culture shift, churches in general were experiencing a major shift. Evangelicalism's engagement with culture and general culture's obsession with both mechanization and business models of success gave way to rafts of new thinking in church. *Discipleship* became the hot-button word along with *church growth*, and everything was systematically measured.[41]

So, what happens when you've got a youth group that's (now) resourced and has its own identity, and a church that's enamored with systems and measurements? Youth Ministry 2.0 allowed culture to inform its **models** and **success**. I realize this is a fairly negative statement, but let me add that this is the kind of youth ministry I grew up in and loved, and it's the kind of youth ministry I led as a youth pastor for many, many years. And we were convinced it was the best response to the culture we lived in. It's a bit like that hot seat I described in the introduction: I'm not exactly sure why we thought it was a good idea at the time, but we were passionately attempting to live out our youth ministry calling amid a general culture and youth culture obsessed with this stuff, and it's what we came up with.

On a more positive note (at least partially positive), the key themes in Youth Ministry 2.0 shifted away from evangelism and correction to **Discipleship** and **Creating a Positive Peer Group**.[42] On a good day, in a good youth ministry, this was about helping teenagers, in the context of community, form their spiritual lives in Christ. The dark side was the creation of the youth group that exists only for itself (which is, unfortunately, still all too common). And while the shift to the theme of Creating a Positive Peer Group might sound like an affinity push, this theme was more driven by the priority of autonomy. Youth workers clamored to develop youth-y churches-within-churches that were loosely attached to, but functionally separate (and autonomous) from, the church that housed and funded them.

Revolutionary ideas about connecting with teenagers in real ways got commoditized (Youth Specialties played a leading role in this), and Youth Ministry 2.0 became

Program-Driven. The sense was—and remains, as I contend—that if we can build the right program with the coolest youth room and hip adult leaders and lots of great stuff to attract kids, then we'll experience success.

In a sense, one could almost subdivide Youth Ministry 2.0 into two parts. The revolutionaries who moved us out of Youth Ministry 1.0 *used* these programs and methods to provide a context for meaningful relationships with teenagers. But rather quickly, the programs and methods became king, and the only real measurement of success anyone in youth ministry cared about was, "How many kids are coming?"[43]

If I can be so bold as to choose a theme verse for Youth Ministry 2.0, it would be *Field of Dreams* 2:32:

> *If you build it, they will come.*

I clearly remember being a high school senior in the youth group of my family's church. I was interested in youth ministry as a career, so I had the privilege of meeting on a semi-regular basis with my youth pastor. During those meetings, he admitted that he was feeling frustrated about our group. We had a great, close-knit youth group... but my youth pastor was always a bit dissatisfied because he felt like we were still missing something. We had great programs, a talented praise band, a top-notch staff of volunteer youth leaders, and students eager to be involved. But some days it seemed like it was all about the youth group, and not so much about those outside our group.

My youth pastor came from the very evangelistic Youth Ministry 1.0, and the "inviting others in" aspect of evangelism was definitely missing from our Youth Ministry 2.0 model. Looking back, I think it's safe to say that my youth pastor was longing for something in the past, dissatisfied about the present state of the youth ministry—and not sure what to do next. How many of us are still feeling this unrest, years later? —*Ben*

I was a true believer in "If you build it, they will come." It sounds wonderful in a world consumed by marketing our niches to get the desired outcome. The problem is that it doesn't work. I realize now that the "If you" was all me—not God. God is missing in the Field of Dreams I build. By grace God showed up in the stuff I built, but now I see that what God built is the only thing that's made any lasting impact. —Jerry Watts

I think your reference to the Great Commission provides the argument AGAINST Youth Ministry 2.0. The resurrected Christ sends his disciples into the dangerous places of the world to make disciples. If I understand you correctly, Youth Ministry 2.0 was more about making the church building bigger, newer, and cooler so people would come to church...but there didn't seem to be an emphasis on doing ministry "in the trenches." —Erik U.

"How many kids are coming?" Parental advisors constantly ask me that question. And this seems to be directly tied to how well I'm doing my job. It's often forgotten that the gospel can be rejected, and maybe the fact that kids aren't showing up means that they're rejecting the gospel.
—Brett Stuvland

Okay, how about an actual Bible verse—the Great Commission, straight from the mouth of Jesus in Matthew 28:19-20a:

Therefore go and make disciples of all nations, baptizing them in the name of the Father and of the Son and of the Holy Spirit, and teaching them to obey everything I have commanded you.

Youth Ministry 2.0 was birthed out of revolutionary, positive intentions. And most youth workers (and churches) still have genuinely positive intentions—even though many of us are working with assumptions about youth ministry that are seriously flawed. But rather than spend our time attacking Youth Ministry 2.0, I'd like to keep our focus on the positive intent of youth workers who want teenagers to know Jesus and want to see those teenagers grow as passionate followers of the Jesus they know and love.

Which brings us to the point of this book: The current shift in youth culture that's made Youth Ministry 2.0 obsolete, whether or not it was ever a good idea in the first place.

	Youth Ministry 1.0	Youth Ministry 2.0	Youth Ministry 3.0
Youth Culture Fixation	Identity	Autonomy	
Cultural Influence on Youth Ministry	Language and Topics	Models and Success	
Key Themes	Evangelism and Correction	Discipleship and Creating a Positive Peer Group	
Driver	Proclamation	Programs	
Theme Verse	Matthew 7:13-14	Matthew 28:19-20a	

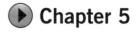

Chapter 5

YOUTH MINISTRY 3.0
NAMING OUR
PREFERRED FUTURE

One of the most dangerous cul-de-sacs that any human organization can drive into is the belief that our current assumptions will continue to be correct, are evergreen, and never need to change.

I'm reminded of a hilarious little video someone sent me a couple of years ago.[44] The video has two people—a man and a woman—quietly riding up an escalator in the massive, but otherwise empty, atrium of a large building. The two characters are spaced about eight steps apart and standing in place as the escalator slowly lifts them to the next floor.

Suddenly, the escalator stops, and the two riders freeze in place.

"Whoa. That's not good," says the man.

"Oh, I don't need this. I'm already late," says the woman.

"Somebody will come. Anybody out there?" says the man.

Then the two, who could easily walk up the few remaining steps, begin expressing the kinds of things they might say if they were trapped in an elevator:

"Somebody?"

"Hell-o?"

(sigh)

"There are two people stuck on an escalator, and we need

help! Now, would somebody please do something?!"

"Help!"

"Well," the man says to the woman as they continue to stand in place, "There's nothing left to do but wait."

This video reminds me of how often our assumptions are completely misplaced. We see the current dropout rates of teenagers after youth ministry, and we assume (with our Youth Ministry 2.0 mindsets), *We need to add cooler programs! We need a big youth center—on the other side of the parking lot from the church! We need better games! We need a state-of-the-art sound system!*[45]

We see kids in our own ministries with shallow, unarticulated faith, and we think, *We need a better curriculum! We need more mission trips to shock them! We need a small groups program—let's see how SaddleCreek does it! We need to increase the youth budget so we can do better stuff or hire a dozen interns!*

Alas. Our thinking is stuck in—let's face it—the previous millennium.[46] We *cannot* build a great youth ministry to reach Youth Culture 3.0 teenagers with Youth Ministry 2.0 methods or thinking.

Check out this wonderful quote I stumbled upon in another book:

> *A church [that] pitches its*
> *tents without constantly looking out for new horizons,*
> *which does not continually*
> *strike camp,*
> *is being untrue to its calling....*
> *[We must] play down our*
> *longing for certainty,*

accept what is risky,
live by improvisation and
experiment.[47] *—Hans Küng*

Youth Culture 3.0— The Third Wave

A strange and sneaky shift has occurred in Western culture: Youth culture has become the dominant culture. At the very least, youth culture has become the dominant informer and shaper of culture at large. Recent studies have shown that children and teenagers influence *more than half* of all household purchases.[48] Middle-aged and younger parents listen to the same music their teenagers listen to (or, at least, music their teenagers listened to a couple of years ago).[49] Middle-aged women wear low-rider jeans. Middle-aged men (and women) sport the

How does a functional youth group operate when you have the Goth kid sitting next to the home-school kid and the home-school kid sitting next to the youth group make-out-machine?

What we have is a very compartmentalized youth group. As the youth pastor, you're trying to tailor the group to seven different cluster identities while hoping and praying everyone can just get along. Oh, and by the way, during youth group you have to talk about Jesus after dealing with the drama and diversity.

Can there really be unity in the midst of diversity? And how do we model this to the students who hate the skate-punk kids who make fun of them at the lunch table? *—jeremy z*

tattoos their kids long for. It's commonplace to see Boomer and Young X-er men wearing earrings and goatees. Clothing brands cross age barriers. TV and movie celebs are Googled by teenagers and adults alike. Adults are all over Facebook and MySpace.

Sure, there are differences—there always will be. And this is where the shift in adolescent task priority comes into play.

I believe the growing period of adolescence speaks to the confusion present with competing metanarratives. It's present in all of society, and even more in the youth subculture. Which story makes the most sense? This is going on within the individual and within the various tribes and affinity groups.

It seems our ecclesiology (and Youth Ministry 3.0) needs to be formed by a robust (narrative) gospel that answers the basic questions of adolescence and of worldview. Instead of targeting youth and their various subcultures it seems we're calling them to emerge into a new identity, autonomy, and affinity that only the biblical metanarrative can offer. —*phoejil*

Youth has become this uncategorizable group that's evolved right under our noses. Just when we believe we've got them figured out, they change. —*Lindsy*

But at the pop culture level, youth leads the day.

It's a natural progression, really. Once youth culture had its identity roughly formed in the first epoch and put hundreds of stakes in the ground about its otherness in the second epoch (autonomy), youth culture cannot stand by while it becomes completely commoditized and commonplace. That rubs against the essential fabric of adolescence.

So youth culture has done three things:

First, youth culture began to play out on two levels. There's the pop, surface-y level shared by teenagers and adults alike. This is the public face of youth culture. It's the sense that youth culture is more than happy to go on letting adults believe pop-culture stuff is the sum total of youth. This isn't a fake part of youth culture, a cardboard stand-in set to pose and deceive. It really is youth culture; but it's only one aspect.

Second, the nonpublic face of youth culture went underground.[50] Like never before, there's a hidden teenage world that almost all adults have no access to, let alone knowledge of. In his excellent book *Hurt: Inside the World of Today's*

Teenagers, Dr. Chap Clark explains that we adults are *not welcome* in this subterranean world, and the best we can do is sit on the stairs that lead to it and be available to kids passing in and out of it.[51]

I recently took my son to see *The Spiderwick Chronicles*, which was adapted from the best-selling series of children's books (Simon & Schuster Children's Publishing) by the same name. In the movie (and the book), siblings stumble onto a new way of using their eyes, which enables them to see—and participate in—an otherwise hidden world of nymphs, sprites, ogres, and other fantastical creatures that had been living all around them all along. They go through much of the movie engaging, befriending, and battling in this hidden world. Meanwhile, their mother is completely unaware of all of this until the very end of the movie when the children let her in on the secret and help her to see it.

I was struck by this movie as a metaphor for this underground/ hidden aspect of youth culture, with the crucial variable that teenagers don't *want* adults to see (or even know about) their

I've had the privilege (not sure if that's a good word to use here, as the teenage hidden sub-world can be quite dark and oppressive) of entering the sub-world of several of my students. Is it dark? You bet. Scary? Yeah, I'll admit it is. Beyond the redeeming work of God? Absolutely not. As agents of change, we need to be ready to enter into the darkness of our teens' lives and walk them out of the darkness and into the light of God's glory. —Ben

One other thing that this generation has in common, no matter what subgroup they're in, is that they're ready to rally around a cause like being more "green" (earth conservation), "red" (AIDS awareness and research), as well as social justice, livestrong, etc.

This generation of teenagers knows there's something worth living for beyond themselves, but they're struggling with actually defining it...and everything else in our culture says it's all about them. This is where the church can step in and say this feeling of theirs comes from being created to glorify God in everything we are: Our relationships, our jobs, our attitudes, our lives.
—Chris Cummings

private, hidden land. It's absolutely commonplace to them: They live in this world with their friends at all times—or, at least, when they're with their friends. They live in this world sometimes at the exclusion of "above ground" youth culture, and sometimes with it.

Teenagers' constant need to differentiate from the adult world (there's autonomy again!) drives them to new, "other" ways of connecting, coping, and creating. Every time some aspect of youth culture becomes commoditized and mainstream, accepted by adults and culture at large, teenagers tweak it in a new way for themselves or create a whole new category.

Case in point: All Web-watchers and adolescent speculators were still convinced that teenagers were going to continue using email and online chat rooms to connect with each other virtually. But teenagers slid out from under

As youth workers we live and minister in a culture of diversity and contradiction. One minute you can have a conversation with a teenager about faith, life, the universe—as deep and insightful as any conversation with an adult—and the next minute you'll have a bunch of kids rolling on the floor because someone farted. Then you throw in all the culturally diverse groups, and you start to realize that instead of trying to make everyone think and be the same, we have to find common ground in Christ so that whoever your kids are, whatever their tribes, wherever they're from, whatever their musical tastes, we can learn to embrace the tension and bring our differences and variety to a place of communion at the cross.

How else could a slightly (okay, more than slightly) geeky classical-music lover from rural England work and minister with New York City's hip-hop loving youth? Only in Christ. —Tom C

that and embraced instant messaging. Then we adults (who, with our last-millennium thinking, love to assume things will stay the same) were shocked—no one predicted this—that teenagers would slide out from under our assumptions about their IM use and move to texting as the most common form of social networking. As I write this, texting is more important and commonplace to teenagers than placing calls on their cell phones.

Third (and this is closely tied to the move underground), youth culture has splintered. While one *might* have some success at describing *some* of the general characteristics of public youth culture, youth culture (both hidden and public) has shattered and dispersed. In my mind's eye, I picture (computer generated) movie scenes of things exploding in space: All the pieces quickly move out in all directions from the center, then slow their retreat and settle into a loosely held orb of various but distinct parts.

While this splintering may have been driven by the ongoing adolescent need for autonomy, the *result* is a desperate grasp for affinity. In other words, the desire for autonomy was so successful (in a way) that it created an affinity vacuum. A monolithic youth culture (or youth group, for that matter) was no longer able to meet the affinity needs of teenagers.

Get this: There's no one-size-fits-all youth culture anymore. That *did* exist in the first two waves of youth culture. But it's likely that it will never exist again. There was a day in the not-too-distant past when the average high school completely revolved around the football players and cheerleaders.[52] Even kids who were part of the math club knew that football players and cheerleaders were the driving force—youth perfected—in their school.

Today's high schools (and middle schools to a lesser degree, as students are less individuated and still trying on various identities) are a goulash of subcultures. The goth group has no aspirations of emulating or cozying up to the jocks and cheer-nymphs. They're broodily content in their own subculture, working hard to define their shared values, tastes, rules, priorities, language, acceptable and unacceptable behavior patterns, style, and more. The "party hard, study hard" gang will tolerate the froofy cheerbabes at parties, but they don't have much in common with them. Even the geeks are more content than ever in their geekitude, having created an entire subculture of their own as well (and not just a fantasy subculture staged in role-playing games).

With these three tectonic plate movements in youth culture, it's kinda obvious why the prioritization of adolescent tasks would once again reshuffle, isn't it?

With youth culture's identity once again at risk due to the dominance and popularization of all things youth, youth culture began grasping for an identity redefinition. And while the move underground was as much about autonomy as anything else, youth culture once again found itself anchorless and ill-defined. Suddenly **affinity** became the long leg of the three-legged stool. Affinity has become the pathway, in a sense, to identity formation and autonomy.

Finding somewhere to belong has always been important to teenagers. However, in the old scenario, at a macro level, kids either did or didn't belong. Of course, many found a way

> Did you ever see the movie *The Warriors* or *Gangs of New York?* That's what today's youth culture is like. You must join a group—or have no identity.
>
> The church is unfortunately on the back end of accepting students as quickly and without judgment as the groups they end up joining in youth culture (see the Burning Man Web site for evidence). That's why Jesus' incarnational ministry was so cool; he brought all these different people from different groups and helped them forge a new identity in him. They were still fishermen and Pharisees and zealots—but found meaning and identity in Christ. Their main mission changed, and they became "true" fishermen and Pharisees and zealots.
>
> —*aaron*

to belong to something or some group outside the macro level. But in a splintered youth culture, it's easier to find a place to belong (affinity)—and yet the search feels more desperate.

Burning Man is a large, annual festival of sorts that takes place in a remote part of the Black Rock Desert in Nevada (120 miles north of Reno) the week before and including Labor Day weekend. It's Mecca to many West Coast teenagers, college students, and twentysomethings. Not a traditional festival with a program and sponsors and marketing, Burning Man is a DIY festival, part earth-worship, part performance art, part celebration of naturalism, and all party. Big party. It's a no-rules, no-cops, no-parents party.

Check out this framing quote from the official Burning Man Web site:

> *You belong here and you participate.*
> *You're not the weirdest kid in the classroom—*
> *there's always somebody there who's thought*
> *up something you never even considered.*
> *You're there to breathe art.*
> *Imagine an ice sculpture emitting glacial*
> *music—in the desert. Imagine the man, greeting*
> *you, neon and benevolence, watching over the*
> *community. You're here to build a community*
> *that needs you and relies on you.*[53]

A bit trippy and psychedelic, sure. But this "marketing copy" is a siren song proclaiming the opportunity for affinity. "Come, be one of us," could be the most powerful thing a teenager in today's youth culture hears.

One of the things youth workers are really good at is looking back (hindsight is always 20/20) and recognizing where God has worked. We're also really good at making long-term plans and trying to project where God is going to work in and through our events and/or leaders. What we're not good at is taking time to recognize God in the reality of now. We hardly ever look to see what God might be doing today.

How do we explain the reality of God *now* to youth? —*Jeff Smyth*

As the church, are we embracing the youthful spirit of adolescence? Or are we squashing it out? We very possibly are to blame for silencing the songs of our youth— for breaking the toes of our teenage "dancers," telling them to get busy when they finally quiet down, and not making time to pass on our stories to them. —*Ben*

What Should Youth Ministry 3.0 Look Like?

If Youth Ministry 1.0 allowed culture to inform its language and topics, and if Youth Ministry 2.0 allowed culture to inform its methods and measurements of success, then Youth Ministry 3.0 needs to allow culture to inform **contextualization**.

Once again, like good missionaries youth workers need to become contextual specialists. Party planners, programming experts, youth preaching obsessors, growth and measurement gurus, and lowest common denominator systemizers are no longer needed. *What's needed are cultural anthropologists with relational passion.*[54]

Do you see how this frees us? Now our passion and calling to connect teenagers with Jesus gets contextualized—in a sense, as the gospel always has—giving us permission to stop copying the neat youth ministry across the country (or even across town) and to be present with the teenagers God has placed in our midst.

That skill set, that outlook, that passion, will *get us to kids*. It will put us on that stairwell to the splintered youth culture underground.

But then what? Youth ministries need to do more than just get to the stairwell, right? Our calling still involves helping teenagers *move* to a place of Jesus-y transformation, an alignment with the kingdom of God, an affinity with the body of Christ.

This stairwell, however, is where we discern our key themes. Instead of the evangelism[55] and correction themes of Youth Ministry 1.0 or the discipleship and create-a-positive-peer-group[56] themes of Youth Ministry 2.0, we need to embrace the key themes of **Communion** and **Mission**.

Communion

For teenagers desperate to define their identities through affinity, we need to help them experience true community. True community doesn't mean once-a-week, highly programmed youth group meetings. True community *might* take place in the context of a small group—but the practice and programming of small groups *does not* ensure true community. True community is life-on-life, whole life, eating together, sharing journeys, working through difficulties, wrestling with praxis (theology in practice), accountability, safety, openness, serving side by side, cultivating shared passion and holy discontent, mutuality, and a host of other variables.[57] True community *is*

I tried several things I thought would be big hits that turned into big flops. Most of my attempts at affinity and cultural application have met with horrid results. But my wife discovered a gem.

She was fed up with her group of girls. They were noncommittal, rude, and just plain apathetic. She finally asked them why they came to the group, and they mostly played the parental-pressure card. Then she asked them what they wanted—and here's the kick in the gut: They didn't want a community (they already had one), they didn't want fun (theirs was a very affluent community with plenty of that)…

They wanted someone to teach them the Bible. (Scary that they didn't think they were getting that.)

I've actually had amazing success recently with an unplanned youth night where I just open the Bible and start reading. (We do some *Lectio Divina*, too.) No games, no band, no contextualization—just read the Bible and talk to students about what it says.
—*Paul*

not a program. It's not something people sign up for. It's not something we force.

But "community" in and of itself didn't seem to completely capture Youth Ministry 3.0 thematically. I knew there was some aspect still missing. So I described what I was thinking on my blog and asked youth workers to help me find the words. My friend and leading Catholic youth ministry expert D. Scott Miller suggested *communion*, and I instantly knew it captured what I was thinking.[58]

Communion is true community with Christ in the mix. Communion is both the *essence* and the *action* of a Christ community.

Many Youth Ministry 2.0 practitioners would assent to this notion and contend that they are, and have been, striving for this theme. For most, though, I would push back in disagreement. First, communion—as I've described it—has been a less-important goal (at best) in most youth ministries. And second, as I've stated a couple of times already: If it's a program, then it's not the kind of communion I'm talking about.

Mission

Mission and *missional* have become buzzwords in the past few years. I'm concerned they're becoming faddish, which would be a great loss as they're so massively pregnant with truth, value, and scriptural integrity.

In their watershed book *The Shaping of Things to Come*, Michael Frost and Alan Hirsch define *missional* this way:

> *In our view, the church should be missional rather than institutional. The church should define itself in terms of its mission—to take the gospel to and incarnate the gospel within a specific cultural context.*[59]

For our purposes here, let's describe *missional* as joining up with the mission of God in the world.[60]

Mission, in this context, is not about having a purpose statement or mission statement. It's not about being purposeful (although that's not a bad thing) or purpose-driven. And I'm *definitely not* using the word *mission* to describe starting a program of missions. *Mission*, in this context, starts with the assumption that God is already actively working on earth, bringing redemption, restoration, and the transformation of all creation. Therefore, a missional ministry seeks to discern, observe, and identify what's close to the heart of God and where God is already at work—and then *joins up with the work of God already in progress*.

Combine these two themes—communion and mission—and you have a youth ministry that could

Our new youth ministry vision is called Inside Out. The simple idea is that we're to "love first always." Love God with everything we've got, and love our neighbors as ourselves.

Through this, we've actually cut every major program—the only thing we still do is youth group each Sunday night. From here we're building communion with our group and Christ and then seeing where God wants us to work in the world.

It's been a great thing. We've already helped with a high school's prom by providing dresses for those who couldn't afford them, hair, makeup, and nails on the day of, and a three-course meal. We're also renovating a room in a nearby motel where families live six to a room; our room is to hold a free afterschool program for the kids who live in the hotel.

It's so exciting when kids get this idea of missional communion. They may think they want something else, but when they experience missional communion, they know this is IT! —*Chris Cummings*

be described as communion on a mission: A Christ-infused, true community seeking to engage the world in God's redemptive work-in-progress. Can you see how this provides meaning and direction to all three adolescent tasks?

"My identity is a follower of Jesus Christ,
framed in real community with others who have a synergistic,
shared passion
for the work of God in the world."
"My uniqueness (autonomy) is found both in the uniqueness
of my own story, as well as the unique ways in which my
contextualized community seeks to live out faith in Christ,
together and for others."

> By its very nature, youth ministry must constantly renew and recontextulaize itself in order to be on the front edge of culture (which is where adolescents are). Perhaps youth ministry serves a greater purpose than only ministry to youth. Perhaps it prophetically ministers to the whole church.
> —James

"My affinity is with these people,
for these people,
with Christ, and for the active
work of God in the world."

If Youth Ministry 1.0 was proclamation-driven and Youth Ministry 2.0 was program-driven, what do we hope for in Youth Ministry 3.0? As I wrote earlier, the "drivers" for Youth Ministry 1.0 and 2.0 came to me quickly, but I really struggled with this third one.

I considered "missionally-driven," but discarded it when I landed on mission as one of the key themes. I considered "communally-driven," but discarded that when I landed on communion as one of the key themes. For weeks I was stumped. I had ideas floating around in my head, values and words and notions and vibes. But none of them were right. All of them had the scent of Youth Ministry 2.0 thinking wafting around them.

So once again I went to the youth ministry collective, through my blog, and I received a wonderful swarm of suggestions based on the glob of fodder I provided for their consideration. But a few people wrote responses that cut across the grain.[61] They provided a track for my thinking to run down.

Whereas Youth Ministry 1.0 was proclamation-driven and Youth Ministry 2.0 was program-driven, Youth Ministry 3.0 needs to be...**not-driven**. It's time to do away with being driven or driving. That metaphoric language might work for herds of cattle, but it doesn't work for a fluid, missional community.

Instead, let's say: **Present.** Present to the work of God in our lives and in the world. Present to the moment, not just living for a day when we leave a horrible world. Present to one another—to those experiencing communion with us, to those who aren't (yet), and even to those who never will be in our community. Present to life in the way of Jesus.[62]

> I was actually planning on coming up with a cool name for the times our group hangs out, but now I think I'll just call it, "Hey, let's meet up this Friday night for dinner at my place." The intention is that "meeting up" not only become synonymous with being together and having great times and laughs but also talking about God, encouraging one another, praying for one another, and discussing Bible questions. Eventually there will be no disconnect between "hanging out" and youth group—because every time we hang out, we'll actually be *having* youth group.
>
> Anyway, I'll definitely go slower on the programs, the cool names, the discipleship workbooks, the events, and get more into just "meeting up." —*Yew Juan*

On one hand, I'd like to choose *the whole Bible* as the "theme verse" for Youth Ministry 3.0, as the very notion of picking a theme verse is a bit reflective of the mechanistic, systematic, programmatic approaches of Youth Ministry 2.0 and the church in general over the last 50 years. But I'll play along with the framework I started with—and I need two verses this time (humor me). From Acts 2:44-46a:

All the believers were together and had everything in common.
They sold property and possessions to give to anyone
who had a need.
Every day they continued to meet together in the
temple courts.
They broke bread in their homes and ate together with
glad and sincere hearts...

There's the communion part. And for the mission part, Jesus' words from John 17:18:

As you sent me into the world, I have sent them into the world.

	Youth Ministry 1.0	Youth Ministry 2.0	Youth Ministry 3.0
Youth Culture Fixation	Identity	Autonomy	Affinity
Cultural Influence on Youth Ministry	Language and Topics	Models and Success	Contextualization
Key Themes	Evangelism and Correction	Discipleship and Creating a Positive Peer Group	Communion and Mission
Driver	Proclamation	Programs	Not Driven, but Present
Theme Verse	Matthew 7:13-14	Matthew 28:19-20a	Acts 2:44-46a, John 17:18

After more than a dozen years in paid youth ministry, my day job for the last decade has been at Youth Specialties. And I've also been a volunteer youth worker in the middle school ministry at my church.

In a sense, I'm the worst youth ministry volunteer on our team. I'm the kind of volunteer who gave me fits when I was the paid guy. I can't do it all. I'd stink at everything if I tried to do it all. So I rarely go on Sunday mornings. I don't go to the events. I rarely go to meetings. I've decided that, with my limited time, my youth ministry will be the best contextual, missional, communional ministry of spiritually transforming relationships I can possibly have with the six students in my eighth-grade guys small group. But I feel as though I'm just scratching the surface of the change that needs to happen—the change that needs to happen in youth ministries across the Western world, as well as in my own little group.

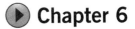

Chapter 6

A word of caution: Sometimes when we move between cultures, things get lost in the process.

Some of this loss is good and natural, but some of it is unfortunate. We need to be extra thoughtful at this juncture in our youth ministry history.

So...

You're a youth worker employed by a church, and you have all kinds of competing demands and expectations you must meet if you want to keep your job.

Real change seems to come during crises. The church isn't exempt from this. —*pbj*

The struggle that many youth workers, including myself, are having is that we've always looked at someone else's group or read the next new book about the top-10 best ways to build a youth program. Too many of us for too long have used others' material and programs and curriculum as a crutch. But programs don't work. And there is no longer "a way"— we must simply seek God's heart and hear from God on what we're each supposed to do in our own contexts.

Our mission statement with the new vision in our youth ministry is to learn to see the world as God sees it, so that we might love the world as God loves it.
—*Chris Cummings*

Real change will need backup from those around you and those above you. It would seem necessary to paint a "macro" picture for everyone, get buy-in, and then plot the implementation on the micro. Then when the speed bumps come, you're not standing alone. —*Mark Allen*

Or you're a volunteer youth worker who'd love to bring change to your youth ministry, but you have limited time and extremely limited clout.

Or you're a senior pastor or other church leader who'd love to see your youth ministry move toward Youth Ministry 3.0, but you're smart enough to know that you can't just write a memo or demand it and expect real change.

So what will this change look like? Assuming some level of agreement with what I've proposed in the last chapter, you've likely taken off in a plane of thoughts and ideas that are (mostly) at the 30,000-foot level. But how to land that plane is a different question.

And, I have to admit: I don't know. It might be a smooth landing, but I doubt it. I think it's more likely to be rough and spine jarring. We're going to have to work this stuff out in the coming years through radical experimentation, glorious failures, unfortunate rabbit trails, ticked-off parents, decreasing numbers, and a host of other challenging—but 100 percent necessary—speed bumps. Speed bumps (or as my friends in the UK call them, "speed humps") are needed right now. All those seemingly ugly things I just listed? We need to welcome them. They'll provide course correction, refinement, pushback, and creative tension.

One thing I'm sure of: Tweaking things won't get us there. Youth Ministry 3.0 isn't about making a subtle modification in one of your programs or adding the words *communion* and *mission* to your youth ministry's core values. Real change is absolutely messy. Always.

But which is better: Messy substantive change or useless mini-alterations?

Nevertheless, I'll take a few stabs at describing some variables of Youth Ministry 3.0.

Contextualize

Before a foreign missionary (or any cross-cultural missionary) hits the ground in a new culture, she spends months or even years studying that culture: Language, customs, beliefs, practices, food, clothes, music and other cultural art, political systems and other systems of power, needs, relational dynamics and family systems, and much more.[64] When she lands, she continues as a student of that culture, learning substantially more when she's living in the actual cross-cultural context. Without this learning, and the logical contextualization of both message and methods that should come from it, she will fail at her mission (at best) or inflict great damage (at worst). Without this learning and the intentional contextualization that flows from it, she will be a colonizer.[65]

In a sense, we've endorsed colonization in youth ministry for decades. But this damaging and fruitless approach has never been as much of a misstep as it is today, with youth culture embodying a deeper otherness than it has in previous decades.

Most youth workers don't have the luxury of studying youth and youth culture (again: Language, customs, beliefs, practices, food, clothes, music and other cultural art, political systems and other systems of power, needs, relational dynamics and family systems, and much more) *prior* to engaging with real teenagers.[66] Most of us need on-the-job training, in-the-trenches learning, and lifelong education. I had wonderful undergraduate and graduate training in educational ministries and curriculum development, cross-cultural education, adolescent development and psychology, theology, and a host of other related topics. And it provided me with a good basis for getting going in youth ministry. But I'd have to say that 90 percent of what I know and practice in youth ministry today has come from learning that happened *outside* of my formal preparation.

And, really, a good cultural anthropologist doesn't just read books about a people group or culture. To borrow the wonderful words of Eugene Peterson's spin on Christ's ministry on earth, referring to the incarnation: She "moves into the neighborhood."

The Word became flesh and blood,
and moved into the neighborhood.
We saw the glory with our own eyes,
the one-of-a-kind glory,
like Father, like Son,
Generous inside and out,
true from start to finish.

—John 1:14, *The Message*

This is key: A "moving into the neighborhood" mindset and practice. We must live incarnationally, positioning ourselves humbly and openly on the sometimes cold, dark, and scary stairwell to the underground of youth culture.

"Believe me: I am in my Father and my Father is in me. If you can't believe that, believe what you see— these works. The person who trusts me will not only do what I'm doing but even greater things, because I, on my way to the Father, am giving you the same work to do that I've been doing...A loveless world," said Jesus, "is a sightless world. If anyone loves me, he will carefully keep my word and my Father will love him— we'll move right into the neighborhood! Not loving me means not keeping my words. The message you are hearing isn't mine. It's the message of the Father who sent me." (John 14:11-12, 23-24, *The Message*)

But it's not just about being a student of youth culture in general. Youth workers committed to a Youth Ministry 3.0 ideal don't move into a conceptual neighborhood. They move into a real neighborhood—with living, breathing, moody, irrational, finicky, guarded, and hurt teenagers! I'm not saying you have to physically relocate your residence. I'm saying that a commitment to contextualization moves us—incarnationally—into the lives of a group of *real* students, not hypothetical ones.

Youth Ministry 3.0 in your context *should* look different than Youth Ministry 3.0 in the church down the street and certainly different than either the church across the country or the denominational norms or the big ol' Youth Ministry

This can only happen when youth ministers and the churches they're a part of change an underlying assumption—that they have something to "teach" youth. Youth Ministry 3.0 assumes that youth are heading to a destination, and that youth ministers are going to the same place. Therefore youth ministries that operate as if they have products or services to impart ought to transition to viewing themselves on a journey alongside youth.
—*Adam Lehman*

These words here are affirming to me as I minister in an entirely different context than any of my friends at the "big churches." I cannot compare my church to theirs, because they are entirely different. Instead of comparing, I just need to stop and look at my church and celebrate the fact that our youth, even if there are fewer than 20 in our group, are making solid connections with adults in our church—and together are fervently taking hold of their faith and finding out where they fit in God's story. Now *that* is a cause for celebration—and an end to comparison! —*Ben*

2.0 mega-group that everyone believes you should clone.

Contextualized youth ministry doesn't come from a book or a conference—two things Youth Specialties offers! It comes from discernment. And discernment always involves inquiry, always involves reading and thinking, always involves careful listening, always involves wrestling with questions that might not be answerable, and always involves the Holy Spirit.

In addition, discernment for contextualization is always better accomplished by a group than by an individual. Youth Ministry 2.0 was all about top-down leadership. Youth Ministry 3.0 is a shared journey, utilizing a shared discernment process and involving both adults *and* teenagers.[67]

You know your students; you know your community. Dream and discern with them to create a localized ministry that brings the gospel to the real kids you see every week.

Wrestle with Three Options

The splintering of youth culture has created a huge method-ological quagmire for youth workers, especially those steeped in "the right program is the answer" thinking. You choose a band for a big youth event (or even put on a CD in your youth group room), and at least half of the teenagers will think it's lame. Some will love messy games and goofy crowdbreakers because the actions and weirdness associated with them fit within the acceptable boundaries of their subcultural norms. Others will hate them, and forcing kids to participate is usually more about us than them. Some kids would love to experience a discipleship process that encourages them to dig into a meaty study, using various online and printed resources, and have feisty discussions about what it means to follow Jesus. Others would find this approach a total disconnect. I could give 20 more examples.

After reading that last paragraph, some of you are surely thinking, *Well, that's the way it's always been. But all kids love games and crowdbreakers if you can get past their tough exteriors. And all real disciples, of any age, should learn to master Bible study techniques like those.*

Says who? Says *you*? (Well, that sure violates the very notion of contextualized discernment.) Says a bunch of really smart youth workers from previous decades, or a bunch of really smart Bible study champs from previous centuries? (Uh, do I really need to respond to that?)

The point isn't just that my small group of white, suburban, eighth-grade boys needs a different approach to youth ministry than the middle schoolers in my friend Christian Dashiell's inner-city group in Kansas City. That's obvious—and it's been so for a long time. The point is that my group of white, suburban, eighth-grade boys needs a different approach to youth ministry than your group of white, suburban, eighth-grade boys! They need a different youth ministry than *any other* group of six kids, even if they look the same on the outside. Youth culture has splintered, so our approaches to youth ministry need to likewise splinter.

So how do we consider going about this? I believe there are three options, which—big surprise—your communional, missional group needs to discern *together*.

Multiple Youth Ministries to Multiple Subcultures

One youth ministry will likely reach only one kind of kid, one subculture. Multiple youth ministries within the same church have the opportunity to establish contextualized, present (not-driven) ministries of communion and mission in multiple youth culture contexts.

I'm not talking about merely having different affinity-based small groups (although that's not necessarily a bad idea) but separate youth groups. There would still be one team, of sorts, with leaders and students from the various groups meeting together regularly for prayer and discernment. But the youth groups would function somewhat autonomously, with their own unique methods, approaches, meeting times, rules, styles, calendars, and shared leadership.

Some might still love the lock-ins, ski trips, and other youth

> One other concern that comes to my mind is that youth are in a state of finding themselves, and many find themselves changing subcultures over the course of a few years. Therefore, would the youth ministry need to constantly change to keep up? Or would that kind of subculture ministry potentially harm students by keeping them in a box, of sorts, in which the people they've developed into (so far) don't actually fit?
> —Ryan Donovan

ministry "technology" of lore; but others would likely develop a highly relational social network online with a swarm approach to meetings—no calendars posted on refrigerators, just the natural lines of connection that exist in teenagers' lives.[68] One group might best accomplish discipleship while meeting weekly to hand out sandwiches to homeless people; another group might approach this in a closed room in the church, with leather-clad Bibles and minds of inquiry.

No great effort would be made to collate all the activities of all of these youth ministries upon one centralized calendar (with the notion that kids need to see a "menu" from which to pick). Anything centralized is anathema to this approach, and picking from a menu is a consumeristic mindset that reeks of Youth Ministry 2.0. Instead, teenagers find their ways to these different groups just as they do in their real, everyday, underground lives: Through social networking.

Teenagers, by the way, may very well choose to participate actively or partially in more than one of these youth ministries. Those few adults and students who have a macro-level view of

> I believe that creating different youth ministries to reach all the types of students will only deepen the rivers of disunity associated with denominations, race, and socioeconomic status. The kingdom of God is made up of all colors, all languages, and all subcultures.
> —*Adam Lehman*

> We have eight off-the-chart adult leaders. All of them have people with whom they connect and meet regularly outside our normal meetings. When we all meet together, it's just for eating and some form of inaugurating God's presence (might be a prayer night, *Lectio Divina*, sermon, devotional, worship—we mix it up). When our adult leaders meet in their groups, they do all sorts of stuff—some affinity-oriented, some spiritual. So far, that's working pretty well.
> I love the way you're describing the paradigm, though—that what works for one group sends the other groups running. I've definitely seen that in the churches I've been in. —*Paul*

the whole thing could assist teenagers who don't know how to engage or where to engage.

This collection of youth ministries doesn't try to be all things to all teenagers. It might not be limited to one church even. (Wouldn't *that* be cool?) Instead, those willing to participate in the process of discernment—and, really, all of the students and leaders—will decide together which youth ministries to birth.

Remember, the church at Berea was different than the church at Corinth. In the "glocal" culture in which we live today, simple geography matters less than affinity and social network.[69]

One Youth Ministry with a Dream of Supra-Culture, Kingdom of God Culture

There's something to be said for gathering together in a community that finds its common affinity in Christ alone. This might be too much to ask of teenagers wrestling with the difficult tasks of adolescence in a culture that has, for the most part, abandoned them.[70] We adults in the church haven't done too well with this: Most of our churches are dominantly homogeneous. But maybe—just maybe—teenagers are the ones who could model a new way for us.

My friend John Wilson, then the youth pastor at Lake Avenue Church in Pasadena, California, brought me in to consult with his paid youth ministry staff on a three-day retreat in the mountains. They felt they were at a turning point in their youth ministry, and they needed to discern a fresh direction and approach. Lake Avenue is a unique church in that it sits at the center of Pasadena, in the San Gabriel Valley, just northeast of Los Angeles. And, in that location, they found more than 50 significant ethnic groups within a five-mile radius of the church. The 100-year-old church had always been predominantly white, with all the worship styles and suburban programming one would expect with that reality. But they were genuinely interested in seeing the congregation move toward reflecting the neighborhood. The youth ministry was passionate about leading the way in this effort.

When we met, they already had a variation on the "multiple youth groups" approach I mentioned above. But it wasn't really working because one group (the white group, with Youth Ministry 2.0 trappings in every way) was the "real" youth group, and the other group (the black and Hispanic kids who'd come in contact with the church through a tutoring program run completely outside the walls of the church) was expected to blend in.

John described one of the tangible problems they were having (which I cite here as an example that goes beyond the more obvious musical tastes and spending potential). The kids from the "neighborhood" youth group didn't divide themselves naturally

Too often we fail to recognize that each of us comes from a cultural background. It's extremely difficult for those from the dominant culture to recognize this—it's kind of like trying to explain water to a fish; it's simply the world in which we live. However, as you rightly pointed out, the great danger is that we can easily assume that our culture is the standard for everyone else, too.

Just as God exists as three distinct persons yet in perfect unity, so too are we called as distinct persons—with unique cultures, ethnicities, and backgrounds—into oneness in community. And this Trinitarian emphasis leads us into the *Missio Dei* concept of being sent into the world, in all our diverse unity.

While ministry can often feel a little bit like dying at times, Youth Ministry 3.0 calls for genuine sacrifice by youth leaders. It's not just about youth leaders investing more time and energy into students but being willing to recognize their own cultural preferences and upbringings along with their students'. This step alone could be revolutionary. Then we can build a kingdom culture that recognizes the worth and validity of each unique cultural identity and points out our deep connectedness in Christ. —*daniel so*

along middle school and high school lines. Their social networks transcended these school-age boundaries. But when they attended the church youth group, they were expected to go one way (high school group) or the other (middle school group), even if it meant separating from their friends.

We worked through a variety of exercises together, praying, dreaming, discerning, and unearthing passion and vision. At one point the team (made up of three white guys—one with a strong passion for the "neighborhood kids"—one white woman, and one Hispanic woman) was a little stuck—until John spoke up with what I can only describe in visionary terms. It felt a little like listening to Dr. Martin Luther King's "I have a dream" speech.

John said something like, "Wait a minute. I want to describe what I'm seeing in the future. I want our youth ministry to be safe for everyone and acknowledge all of these tribes' uniquenesses and values and styles. I want them to move into and through a great place of multiculturalism, based on respect, humility, and valuing each other. But, ultimately, I dream of a day when we can move beyond a multicultural youth group to a kingdom-culture youth group. I want our youth group to feel like heaven."

It was a beautiful vision. Difficult to realize? Absolutely. Worth striving toward, knowing there will be failure and redirects and conflict along the way? Absolutely. The group quickly rallied around this vision and chose to move forward on the two action points (out of a list of dozens) that they thought would most leverage them toward this dream. They put a stake in the ground and said, "We have to hire a black copastor (alongside and equal to the existing high school pastor), no matter what it does to our budget." Each team member found significant areas where they would cut spending, including interns and other highly valued resources, in order to fund this new hire without having to ask the church for more money (which they knew would have been a long, uphill battle). Within months, they'd hired an amazingly gifted black high school pastor who served as an equal on their team.

Their second action was to build a Sunday morning youth worship service—open to all ages and welcoming of families—that was neither middle school nor high school, but both. It also represented aspects of all the cultural and socioeconomic groups represented in their mix. This has proven a more difficult action point and hasn't been fully realized yet. But the dream is still alive.

This dream relates closely to the idea of youth subcultures from different racial and socioeconomic groups coming together into one kingdom-culture. But what might this look like, to have a youth ministry of the various youth subcultures in your church and community, acknowledging the uniqueness and value of each—including the styles and preferences of each—but moving toward a supra-cultural taste of the kingdom of God?

Many, many youth workers would respond, "Well, that's what we have already. At least that's what we *try* to have." In the vast majority of cases, this assumption is flat-out false. Instead, I'd suggest that what you probably have now is what Lake Avenue had before they got intentional about this change:

A one-size-fits-all youth ministry built on either

- the lowest common denominator of all the subcultures in your group, or
- the norms—style, language, music, meeting time preference, meeting format, and so on (see the complete

list a couple pages back)—of one subculture (usually the one representing the parents with the most money and power in the church) and expecting (maybe hoping?) that kids from other subcultures will "grow up" and fit in.

Some Hybrid of the Two

Both of the first two options (multiple youth ministries to multiple subcultures *and* one youth ministry with a dream of supra-culture, kingdom of God culture) are amazing, but it would take a high level of courage and commitment to pull off either one of them. So if the polarity of these first two leaves you convinced that neither one seems feasible, there are some hybrid options that could be considered. At this point I see two, primarily; but I'm sure some communion-centered groups committed to Youth Ministry 3.0 could come up with more:

One group for some stuff; smaller subculture-specific groups for other stuff. Subcultures can come together for some aspects of youth ministry—at least we'd like to believe this is true. Worship could be one of them

In my context, the hybrid approach works best. My students seem to want to be together for fun activities, but separate for the deep, meaty parts of our youth ministry. Some like to gather with other adults in the church to read and discuss books. Some like to meet with either my wife or I at coffeeshops or restaurants and just chat about life. Some love having a youth leader (typically me) visit them at school during lunch.

Christ came to unite us as his body, and at our core, we carry the same mark of God. Some of us, though, differ in how we connect with God and the church. I think it's important to give our students time to be together so that they grasp the fact that the church isn't just full of people like them. But it's also important that we affirm the fact that God has created each one of them uniquely, yet provide opportunities for them to build affinity with others like them—regardless of age.
—*Ben Kraker*

(assuming worship isn't anchored to only one subculture's style preferences). Certain trips—like a mission trip—could be a wonderful place to get kids from different subcultures working alongside each other. Different subcultures are able to come together more easily when they have a common goal, purpose, or task apart from the norm for both (or all) groups. And these "combined" activities could be surrounded by a galaxy of groups functioning more like the description of the multiple youth ministries approach.

One group most of the time, but with some specific, contextualized efforts to create space for the subcultures to which your ministry is called. This hybrid approach shoots for the supra-cultural reality, but it realizes there are some kids who won't fully connect with those options. Therefore various subculture-specific gatherings and efforts are directed—usually by adults who sense callings to those various subcultures—to meet the latter's communion and mission needs within their contexts.

This might look like a communional group that participates in most aspects of the youth ministry together but has one intentional sidecar ministry to kids in the hardcore subculture and another intentional sidecar ministry to social-activist kids who want to dig in deeper to national and international issues and find ways to engage them. To be fair, this is what the Lake Avenue youth ministry has been attempting to do, as they still have their specific ministries to "neighborhood" kids, such as after-school tutoring and events specific to that affinity group.

Here's a likely (and fair) question: "Don't all these approaches you've just described sound as though they'd be possibilities for only a large youth group? What about our youth group of *eight* kids?" I can understand this question (which is why I included it), and you probably expect me to reply, saying, "No, this isn't only for larger groups"—right?

Actually, for a small group, the latter mindset and these approaches might look like one youth leader being intentional about regularly hanging out with the two kids from the emo subculture, entering into their world, getting to know their friends, and creating something together. Or it might look like one leader spending time with *one* kid who's part of the art subculture; again, getting to know her friends and creating something together—likely offsite, apart from the church and difficult to measure.

Caution: Don't allow one youth leader with a Youth Ministry 3.0 mindset and a calling for a particular subculture influence you to leave the rest of your group in a one-size-fits-all Youth Ministry 2.0 context.

Another fair question: "Are you suggesting we care about only those students who are already in our ministry?" I can see why it would be easy to conclude this based on what I've written so far (which is why I thought of the question). But, of course, no, that's not what I'm suggesting. Just the opposite, actually. I'm suggesting that you *start* with the teenagers God has already placed in your midst. Consider how you might do Youth Ministry 3.0 with them first. Then, *along with those students*, discern a contextualized dream for how your youth ministry can look outward.

A contextualized youth ministry that acknowledges different subcultures *should* lead your ministry, naturally, deep into the various social networks that your students work hard to sustain outside of your otherwise cloistered group. Acknowledging that your students' lives are much bigger than youth group (part of the whole-life mindset I mentioned earlier) will lead you, within youth culture, to connect with kids outside your church. This is very different than planning a big, attraction-oriented outreach event and hoping all teenagers will attend: The first humbly and relationally moves outward, the second attempts to create a large sucking vacuum inward.[71]

Do Less

One of the most important, dangerous, and courageous steps that any youth ministry needs to take if it's going to make the shift from Youth Ministry 2.0 to Youth Ministry 3.0 is to cut programs. But this is where it has to start. (Well, after much prayer and dreaming and dialogue, that is.) There's just no way to move to Youth Ministry 3.0 by *adding* more programs. This isn't the way, and it will fail.

> If we take time to really contemplate the idea that God wants people to come to him more than we people to come to him, then we'll start to head toward Youth Ministry 3.0. While I believe a ton of youth ministers (and pastors) agree that "God wants it more than we do," the way they operate ministries would seem to suggest otherwise. —Adam Lehman

Let's be honest about youth ministry: The demands of teenagers' lives, parents' needs, planning, preparation, communication, and everything else that comes with it are overwhelming. And it's absolutely never, ever done. Never completed. There will always be more teenagers who need you. There will always be more parents who'd benefit from time you spend reaching out to them. Your teaching could always be a little better with more prep time. Your pastor and church board will always desire more communication (or acquiescence). So adding more gets you nowhere.

Last summer we had three large trips and events, and I even had two interns—but within it all we realized after the summer was over that we hadn't done YOUTH ministry...we'd done PROGRAM ministry. Through it, kids' lives were not changed (even though the events went well), and we knew then something needed to be different.

Starting in January this year, we announced our new vision of youth ministry and also announced that there would be no large events for one year.

So this is where we are four months later: We're compiling a list of people from our church who want to be mentors; my fiancee and I have started mentoring a few youth already to see what recommendations and suggestions we can make for the mentors in training; finally, all adults who interact with youth have much deeper relationships because of the simplicity of our new schedule.

Doing less has already accomplished so much more when it comes to truly life-changing relationships. —*Chris Cummings*

And *even if you had the time* to add more, doing so is a fool's errand, a wrong turn into a cul-de-sac of misdirection.

The road forward must first go through the valley of doing less. Admittedly, this is counterintuitive. Doing less *feels* like shying away from needs, turning away from change. Society has enculturated us to believe that change comes from doing more, more, more. But even Jesus, the Christ—who certainly, as God incarnate, should have been able to do more stuff than you and I do—stepped aside for prayer and rest and intimate dialogue. And he often did so when the to-do list was at its most substantial and critical.

Strip down your programming so you have space to spend time with teenagers, spend time with God, and consider rebuilding something new and fresh.

Get Small

Remember the Steve Martin bit, "Let's get small"? It was one of the lines that launched him into massive stardom.[72] Of course, Martin was making a "laugh at them while you laugh at me"

joke about drug use. But his advice couldn't be more apropos for those of us trying to embrace Youth Ministry 3.0.

Let me say it plainly: *Large* is part of the value system of Youth Ministry 2.0; small is a cornerstone to Youth Ministry 3.0. Communion necessitates small. Contextualization begs for small. Discernment requires small. Mission is lived out in small.

No, I'm not merely saying that every good youth ministry should add small group programs (although much good has come from the move toward small groups as the primary fabric in many youth ministries). I'm not even sure we should continue using the phrase "small group." It comes with too much baggage, and it instantly brings mental and emotional memories of forced community, programming, and utility.[73]

Smallness is both a value and a practice, though the value has to precede and continue on through the practice. Smallness values community in which teenagers can be truly known and know others,

I'm convinced that small is the way to go. Small lets us focus more effectively on relationships and community. We're actually surrounded by opportunities for relationship, both personal (family, friends, youth groups) and technological (cell phones, facebook, etc.), yet we often still struggle with "being community." (How often has your church talked about ways to be more hospitable?) Recently we changed our senior high ministry focus to home gatherings where we share a meal, have conversation, and hang out together. There's been a good response from the students—they're connecting and getting to know each other better. Growth is happening, even if the attendance is somewhat smaller. There are opportunities to be real with each other and more willingness in this type of context to do so.
—*Chris Nickels*

When I put on an event like '80s bowling or something BIG, I literally get half (if not less) the number of kids that I get on a typical youth night. And not that numbers are the most important measure, but this year I added a whole lot more texting, MySpacing, coffeeshop visits, school visits, and small group visits. And I've noticed a booming youth group this year. Kids feed off authenticity.
—*DanRead*

There's a lot to be said about going small. Sure, Jesus had the mega-services where he preached to the masses, but his time with his core group of three should be underscored as most important. Why are we convinced that more time, energy, and resources should be invested in our weekend services or programs when, if we invested as much (or more) in our core group we—like Jesus' core—could turn the world upside down? —*Terrace Crawford*

rather than being one of the crowd (even if it's a really fun crowd). Smallness champions clusters of relationships rather than a carpet-bombing approach. Smallness waits on the still, small voice of God rather than assuming what God wants to say and broadcasting it through the best sound system money can buy. Smallness prioritizes relationships over numbers, social networks over programs, uniqueness over homogeneity, and listening to God over speaking for God.

Help Students Experience God

Maybe you've seen this diagram before:

In the second half of the last century, as our systematic, scientific, rational, modern mindset calcified into theology that was assumed to be complete and timeless, many people used this little diagram to explain the relationship of facts and feelings to faith.[74] The explanation goes: Facts—objective truth—are the engine of the Faith Train. Facts are trustworthy and will propel us down the track and always in the right direction. Of course, Faith is the coal car that provides fuel to the engine. And Feelings are the caboose, which can be helpful, but isn't essential to the operation of the train. Similarly, feelings cannot be trusted, and they shouldn't inform faith or facts.

This mental map wasn't unique to the church, but it typified the modern mindset dominant in the Western world from the time of the Enlightenment, propelled by the Reformation and the rise of science and on into the twentieth century (until things such as quantum physics, mistrust of authority, and other factors slowly began to pull at this worldview's king-of-the-hill status).

You can hate postmodernism all you want—even call it every sort of nasty name you like—but the reality is completely indisputable: We live in a postmodern culture.[75,76] Scripture calls us to be *in the world.*[77] If we have any hope of engaging teenagers in their world, then we simply must understand and minister in the context of a postmodern mindset.

Doing less is important, just as doing excellently what we've planned to do is important. Contextualization is only meaningful when the content isn't compromised. Relationships for the sake of relationships aren't part of God's design. Simplification of youth ministry should be twofold: Edifying the saints and building relationships in order to share the gospel. Our methods should change but our message MUST remain the same. —*Ben Bacon*

One of the "problems" that arises by doing less is doing nothing. In the process of doing less, we need to think strategically. I don't think we can just throw stuff against the wall to see if it sticks. And I don't think we can completely remove all programs. Many groups are run by volunteers who're just as busy as students and families—they need help building relationships with kids. So, if done well, there can be benefits to "programming" small groups, mentoring, large group events, etc. —*RO Smith*

I agree that authenticity and relationship trump programs...but for us I think it's more of a both-and rather than an either-or. Simply doing less and getting little is not enough—especially for churches with naturally big ministries. I think we have to learn to be "little" big churches. —*brandon*

Here's how the little train of modernism has had its cars rearranged:

While the culture may allow us to make facts the caboose, I don't think that's an adequate position for facts. And maybe the word *fact* is part of the problem. The very word implies textbook responses and cold systematic answers. Instead, maybe we should scrap *facts* and replace them with *truth*.

If we settle on *truth* as the new *facts*, however, we cannot relegate it to the caboose. Resigning truth to the back of the train very well may leave us with a derailment down the road. This is because experiences not based deeply in truth have a tendency to veer off course. Instead maybe truth needs to become the tracks on which the whole train moves. In this way our experiences and the faith that fuels them rest on a well-maintained foundation that can prevent us from derailing. Truth is the one thing that separates the train we have to offer from all the other faith trains out there.

—*Luke Angus*

Faith is still the fuel, but in a postmodern world, most teenagers (not all) come to a place of faith through their experience of the Divine in others, in themselves, in nature, in spiritual community, in Scripture, in popular media, in pain, with the poor and mistreated, and through all of the other myriad places where God can be actively found. This experience (which always has an intimate relationship with feelings) becomes a pathway to faith. However, facts are still there. Actually, it might be fair to say the caboose is more important in this scenario, but facts support faith and validate experience.

With this reality in mind, Youth Ministry 3.0 needs to be intentionally proactive about providing teenagers with opportunities to experience God, not merely hear facts about God. What does this look like? In a word: Worship.

But let me remind you of a little scriptural gadfly about worship:

[God says,] "I hate, I despise your religious festivals;
I cannot stand your assemblies.
Even though you bring me burnt offerings and grain offerings,
I will not accept them.
Though you bring choice fellowship offerings,
I will have no regard for them.
Away with the noise of your songs!
I will not listen to the music of your harps.
But let justice roll on like a river, righteousness like a never-failing stream!" (Amos 5:21-24)

Yes, worship includes the experience of raising our voices together in songs to God. And, yes, worship involves prayer. But a broader—more scriptural—view of worship is about serving the poor, righting injustice, caring

Adolescents demand more than observer status in almost every conceivable facet of life today. They don't just want to watch TV; they want to vote on the outcome. They don't just want to download videos; they want to create them. They don't just want to be listed in directories; they want to shape their own profiles. In short, they demand experiences. Is it really any surprise that they begin to doubt when the church doesn't provide an experience of the living God? —*Kevin*

Young people (and adults) don't need knowledge of God or feelings about God; they need to encounter God. They need to experience God in a tangible way that in turn creates feelings, knowledge, and faith. Their faith isn't rooted in the way they feel about it or the facts they've memorized; it's rooted in their own eyewitness accounts. —*Chris Marsden*

Why is it so easy to "create" worshipful experiences for our students, yet so difficult for us to personally experience the Divine? If Youth Ministry 3.0 is to succeed, we must personally experience the divine—not just on our own time, not just with our youth, but all of the above as the greater church body. —*Ben Kraker*

for those in need. When teenagers—whether they're already followers of Jesus or not—*experience* this kind of worship-in-action, they have an enormous opportunity to have a tangible *experience* of God in their lives. This often leads to faith (or more faith). More importantly, this leads to a *sustainable faith.*

Funny, isn't it? The first train diagram told us that feelings do not lead us to a sustainable faith, since feelings can't be trusted. Maybe that was true 50 years ago. I'm not sure. But I'm sure of this, though: For today's teenagers, *experience is what they trust.* And, if we're really honest, this is how we all live.[78]

These experiences of the Divine become sustaining markers in the journey of an adolescent, more than a robust factual knowledge base could ever be. When a teenager is sitting in third-period science class and hearing arguments that might undermine her factual knowledge (as strong as that may be), it will be her experience of God—last week in her spiritual community, last month in the soup kitchen, and last summer on the mission trip—that sustains her faith in the face of seemingly objective facts to the contrary.

I'm having a little bit of trouble here with your proposition. An appropriate response to the gospel is faith or trust in Jesus Christ and facts about who he is and what he's done on the cross. If we allow feelings to lead the train, our feelings can lead us all over the place because of our sinfulness. It's not feeling that Scripture calls us to but faith in an objective reality outside ourselves. If all we listen to are feelings or inner voices or experiences, we get a wide range of ideas that may or may not fit the biblical truth God revealed to us. As teenagers experience truth in Scripture accompanied by the power of the Holy Spirit, their emotions or feelings will come in joyous waves. —*Jason Pittman*

Be Communional

I've used the word *communional* in this book a few times now, so it's time for me to 'fess up: I made it up. But I believe it's a good word, and we should make it part of our lexicon of Youth Ministry 3.0.

Communional is the adjective form of the word *communion*. It implies an intentional state of being. If I'd merely written "build community," then it would likely take us down the Youth Ministry 2.0 highway to things such as:

- Manipulatively forcing "community" onto teenagers;
- Constructing new programs for community;
- Assuming that hanging out together (even in a spiritual context) is the same thing as community;
- Utilizing tricks of the trade to lure kids into community.

Communion doesn't occur because of well-thought-out programs or sleight of hand or being in the same room. Communion is the organic, unmanipulated, fluid,

I'm in the metro Washington, D.C., area. Very, very busy. Eight years ago we dropped our weekly youth meeting. None. We strengthened our weekly Sunday school class (a lot) and strengthened once-a-month youth ministry events. I don't miss the weekly grind of producing a program that'll be forgotten by the next morning. The youth don't miss a weekly meeting. And none of the parents miss the hassle of driving through traffic weekly even though their presence is required at the monthly events. While their responsibility of being the lead spiritual influencers on their own children (as well as the other teens) has increased greatly, no one complains. —*Brenda Seefeldt*

Moving away from programs often means moving away from what we've conjured up as our security. But when we do become less programmed and then more insecure, we begin to discover where we should really be finding our security.

True security is found in things that last; apart from God, it's found primarily in relationships with others in the church. The really neat thing is that we have the opportunity to discover security (and intimacy, unconditional love, and a whole host of other benefits) alongside our youth, our leaders, and ideally, churchgoers from every generation you mentioned. —*Ben Kraker*

Communion is small, but it demands a larger perspective. One who experiences "communion" senses connection to the larger body of Christ when it assembles as the church—as well as the Christ-hungry in Africa or Christ-oppressed in Tibet. Communion is slow, simple, fluid. In other words, good luck programming the working of the Spirit in others. As a matter of fact, why try? You risk only getting in the way. Communion is present. So look around —where are your adult volunteers? Can you possibly ever have enough? Don't they need/deserve better training for face time, listening, and shared experience? Seriously, Mr. Lone Ranger, sir, if you are the end-all, be-all of adult presence to young people in your church, you're not ready for the future. We need an adult church with a missional mindset that includes teenagers, and we need teenagers with a missional mindset within the church. Communion is Jesus-y. Come to think of it, communion was the Jesus-y stuff that became the reason I got into youth ministry in the first place. —*D. Scott Miller*

and difficult-to-quantify shared fruit of consistent relationships with Christ in the mix. (Yes, it's organic fruit!)[79]

A few aspects of communion:

Communion is small. I already wrote a whole section on small, so I won't harp on it here. But it bears repeating that communion rarely, if ever, occurs in a large setting.

Communion is slow. It's not rushed. It doesn't happen overnight—in fact, it's annoyingly patient. Communion doesn't happen on our timetables at all, and it will internally resist all forms of quantification.

Communion is simple. Not simple to "create," but simple in its DNA. It's not flashy. It doesn't flourish with booster shots of technology.[80]

Communion is fluid. It won't be boxed and sold as a resource or presented as a 40-day plan. It shies away from being defined. It beautifully morphs into variant vibes, seasons, and shapes.

Communion is present. It demands face time. It hungers for listening. It salivates for shared experience. It lives in the here and now.

Communion is Jesus-y.[81] It places high value on the expectation of God showing up. It notices Christ in our midst. It seeks to live out a shared experience of joining up with the redemptive work of Christ.

Youth Ministry 3.0 shares the Jesus life with your community of students, the "we're in this together-ness" of real communion, dependent on the reality of God in your midst.

Work Toward Integration of Teenagers with the Church

Much has been written in the last decade about "Family-Based Youth Ministry." (Although, if I'm honest, much of this has merely been the addition of a couple events to an already program-driven approach to youth ministry.) Not that understanding teenagers as part of a family system and ministering to their parents aren't important—of course they are. But what I'm suggesting here is larger and broader.

The fact is, teenagers *need* adults in their lives—multiple adults. But the church also needs teenagers. Blue Hairs need Kindergarteners; Teenagers need Empty Nesters; Twentysomethings need Boomers. We're all the church, like it or not, and the *choice* to like it is a critical one.

Isolated youth groups have done just as much harm as good. Isolation might make things easier in some ways, but striving for the best is rarely easy.

Work to find meaningful ways for intergenerational community and relationships. Find meaningful ways for adults of all ages to connect to the work of the youth ministry and attempt (with noble failure being a necessary part of the process) to find paths for integrating teenagers into the lives of adults in your church.

It sounds like bumper-sticker theology, but it's so very true for Youth Ministry 3.0: We all need each other.

Be a Missionary

Early on in youth ministry, one of my biggest misconceptions was that it was my role to be a buddy to teenagers. My faulty logic told me that if I succeeded in becoming one of them—a peer—then I'd have access to influence their lives to a greater degree. It wasn't until I discovered that I'd accomplished this that I saw the folly of my thinking. I'd forfeited my place as a mentor in order to become a pal.

Missionaries don't pretend to be one and the same as the people they're living with and ministering to. How fake and offensive would that be? Instead, they humbly and cautiously engage with people, being ever thoughtful and caring about cultural context, while acknowledging their own visitor status. Even the great missionary stories of the last century in which the missionaries reached a beautiful place of being an accepted part of a tribal culture still bore this reality: No matter how much the tribe loved, appreciated, and accepted them, they were still the alien who was "other." (*Bruchko*[82] and *Peace Child*[83] made a massive impression on me when I read them as a teenager.)

I'll say it again: Youth Ministry 3.0 doesn't call for programming experts, systemizers, communication specialists, or party planners. Youth Ministry 3.0 calls for anthropologically minded missionaries who serve teenagers with humility and grace.

Help Students Be Missional

Having already defined *missional* as joining up with the mission of God in the world, I want to parse the concept a bit in order to move toward practical application. Joining up with the mission of God in the world sounds good and all, but it could leave youth workers who resonate with this a bit like a dragster with no tires—revving the engine, but with no means of going anywhere.

Joining up with God's mission in the world *can* happen without intention. Students may suddenly find themselves (or we may suddenly find ourselves) in the midst of some action or effort or people in which the presence of God is palpable. And in that moment, they'll know (because they *feel* it—ahem) they've stumbled into the movement of God, and they're just along for the ride.

We need to help our teenagers watch for these moments—and we all experience them.

But most youth ministry doesn't happen this way. Most communional groups need to *choose* to be missional, *choose* to find the active work of God. In most cases, this takes a re-orientation of our vision. This is particularly true for teenagers who (because of the massive quantity of change going on in their bodies, minds, and lives) are naturally, and understandably, self-focused. Opening their eyes and minds and hearts to others is a huge step, a big shift, and a wonderful disequilibrating opportunity.[84]

I found a wonderfully helpful unpacking of real change in a new-agey business book called *Presence: Human Purpose and the Field of the Future*.[85] The authors contend that deep and lasting change (for an organization or an individual) entails seven stages in three phases. They call this diagram "the U" because the first three stages are a tearing down or deconstruction of what was, and the last four stages are a rebuilding or reconstruction.

Here's a chart of the "U" from page 225 of the book.[86]

Seven Capacities of the U Movement

The entire U movement arises from seven core capacities and the activities they enable. Each capacity is a gateway to the next activity—the capacity for suspending enables seeing our seeing, and the capacity for prototyping enables enacting living microcosms—but only as all seven capacities are developed is the movement through the entire process possible.

I'd like to grossly paraphrase their brilliant work, shifting it into four stages (two down, and two up):

1. Stage one (the first half of the downward side of the U) is a **naming of the current reality.** This is a gut-check honest

acknowledgment of observed, sensed, discerned, or revealed truth (or, likely, some combination of those).

For a teenager on her first Friday night with a group of kids who hand out sandwiches and engage in conversation with homeless people, this first stage could look like the disequilibrating "a-ha!" that says homeless people are real people with real stories and emotions, not merely dirty, two-dimensional scenery that needs to be cleaned up.[87]

2. The second stage of deep change (the bottom half of the downward side of the U) is the hard work of **deconstruction**. Naming the current reality creates a gap between itself and the previously held assumptions or beliefs. Then these previously held assumptions or beliefs must be torn down, to one extent or another, before any rebuilding can occur.

Can't you see how this happens in your own life? Think of it as a house remodel. We can't get to "a whole new look" before going through the dusty, messy, annoying (and sometimes costly) task of cleaning out, clearing away, ripping down, dismantling, and discarding the old stuff.

For that teenager we met a few paragraphs ago, this second step takes place through weeks of continued involvement in this ministry, hearing more stories of homeless people, having some of them remember her name and her remembering their names, engaging in multiple discussions with her friends and leaders about what she'd previously and incorrectly assumed or believed, and hours spent thinking on her own.

3. Now comes the work of rebuilding. Stage three of the U (the bottom section of the upswing on the U) is the conscious or subconscious act of **naming a new reality**. This articulation

is much more complex and dimensional than would have been possible in the first stage. And, instead of a naming that's connected to misunderstanding, this is a naming connected to hope and a new vision. This is "stake in the ground" stuff.

For our teenager, this is a lengthy process of formulating new opinions and vocabulary, emotional responses and commitment about, for, and to the homeless people she has come to know. (Can you see how this fits with the identity, autonomy, and affinity tasks we've already talked about so much in this book?)

4. Finally, we get to stage four (the top half of the upswing on the U), which is the **practical living out** of this new belief and understanding. If action hasn't occurred yet, it sure does at this point. Behaviors and choices are modified in response to this new perspective, understanding, and commitment.

Our teenager, who's been living all of this out in her actions since that first evening with the homeless, now has the wherewithal to make informed choices and take proactive steps without being told what to do. She has a confidence about her involvement in this missional work because it's become a part of her belief system, part of her identity. (Of course, the group with whom she goes into the city each week has also grown into a strong, communional affinity group for her.)

Other ways we can help students to discover and join up with God's work in the world are:

- Regularly share stories, and ask teenagers to share stories, of places where you "caught a glimpse of God." Allow this storytelling to become natural and normative in your group.
- Encourage your students with the biblical reality that the earth is God's, and everything in it.[88] The natural

extension of this truth is that God can be found, living and active, all over the place. Since all of us are God's creations, even those who aren't intentionally following Jesus will leak out bits of the gospel in art, film, music, print, conversation, and other public arenas. Constantly ask your students—while standing in a forest or on a mountaintop or in the middle of a slum or in the parking lot of their school—"What can we learn about God from this place?" and "Where and how is God present in this place?"

- Together, learn about various injustices in your community, your region, your country, and the world. Together, discern your individual and collective "holy discontent" and devise a way to address that issue.
- Try a wide variety of missional activities and—together—discern where God is moving you or calling you.

Help teenagers see God's calling on their lives to discover where God is doing something and give their lives to it.

Finally, Don't Be Driven

I'm a big fan of passion—both the concept and the experience. I've probably chosen passion as a speaking theme to both teenagers and adults more than any other subject over the last 10 years. I believe that Jesus' promise in John 10:10—*I have come that they may have life, and have it to the full*—is one of the most inspiring and wonderful verses in all of Scripture.

But I've come to believe there's a difference between passion and being driven.[89] Passion calls to us; being driven coerces us. Passion seduces us; being driven guilts us. Passion is invitational; being driven is prescriptive. Passion is inquisitive;

Sadly, I fall into the trap of thinking that if I'm not doing anything ministry related, then I'm not serving God. But the truth is, if we really want to be used by God, then we have to be with God constantly in prayer, in the Scriptures, and in rest. —*Ryan*

I was burned out from trying to maintain a drive-by relationship with God while taking on more and more ministry responsibilities. I'll never forget the words that my mentor shared with me when I came to him and was at my worst:

"Nothing essential stops when I rest."

The world won't fall apart if I take some time to myself. My students will survive without me while I pull away for a short period of time. The church will continue to go on without me.

Those six simple words have become a rule of life for me.
—*Ben Kraker*

My relationship with God and my job at the church must be separate. I'm passionate about both, but when I see them as the same I find myself working more than I can sustain to try to make myself feel holy. And if I'm totally honest, that "holy" feeling only ever comes from my own sense of satisfaction or the praise of other people.
—*Jeremy Best*

being driven is punitive. Passion is full of emotion; being driven is cold and calculating.

Teenagers desperately want to experience passion, but they sure aren't interested in being driven!

And youth workers who embrace a Youth Ministry 3.0 mindset and approach will stop being driven by job descriptions, measurements, buildings, time demands, and Messiah complexes. Instead, we'll slow down enough, deconstruct enough, to be fully present.

First, present to Jesus Christ's activity in our own lives. The nourishment of the soul must become priority number one for youth workers in this new epoch. We simply must stop giving lip service to this while imitating the Road Runner of cartoon fame. (Beep-beep!)

How this personal soul refreshment plays out for each youth worker is, of course, contextual. For my own temperament and tastes, I've found that a quarterly, three-day silent retreat does more for me than a half-day of down time once a week. I'm ruthless about protecting this practice in my life. I find a place where I can prepare my own food (usually someone's cabin or something like that) so I don't even have to make small talk. I turn off my cell phone, leave my computer at home, and completely disconnect for three days. I bring a stack of books, I sleep, I pray, I meditate, and I occasionally journal. Sometimes God meets me in profound ways, and sometimes God reveals new insights concerning me or my relationships or God's character. But often it's just the discipline of slowing down and shutting up that brings the detox and realignment I need.

But we must be present to more than ourselves. We also need to adopt a constant mindset and discipline of presence: To our primary relationships, to the teenagers in our midst, to the beauty of creation, to God's presence all around us. Without presence we might become ignorant to the needs of teenagers. Without presence we might ram our ideas and assumptions onto them rather than waiting and listening for their ideas and assumptions. Without presence, we might only experience a

Parents want driven programs for their kids because that's the world they've given their kids—academics, school sports with too-high expectations in regard to time and energy, band practices every night, no sleep during the school drama, part-time jobs.

To merely *seem reasonable*, church has to fit that mold—not to mention that the only way to ensure that a church event reaches a student is to hold as many events as possible. That way at least one or two of those events will fall into the hole in a particular student's schedule. (I can think of a couple of parents who want me to plan 17 things a week simply on the off chance their children might make one of them!)

To me the big question always goes back to the parents: Are they living their lives with purpose, or are they simply driven? What model is that showing their children?
—*Troy Richards*

I've been living abroad for six years and in countries where I'm usually considered the outsider, especially where I live now in West Africa. Sometimes the only thing I know how to do is be there. I'm not always sure what to say or what to do. But I can listen, maybe smile, and reflect Christ in small ways. One of my African friends once told me, "Africans value solidarity. What is solidarity? Standing together, being all there." Not a bad way to live and serve in ministry.
—*Matt Price*

drive-by relationship with God.

Be present to your calling; present to Christ in you; *present to teenagers and to Christ in them.*

EPILOGUE

As we wrap up this book, I'd like to suggest that Youth Ministry 3.0 calls us, full circle, back to some of the stirrings of the earliest youth workers. Youth Ministry 3.0 calls us back to the margins.

For many years, youth ministry has enjoyed a heyday of growing resources, increasing validation, fine-tuned technology and systems, and an entire industry both supporting and objectifying it. Youth Specialties has been an unwitting but active participant in this process; and for that, I am deeply regretful and sorry.

The Youth Specialties of today and tomorrow, however, will be one of Youth Ministry 3.0—one of encouragement, humility, trailblazing, and a few potentially prophetic nudges.

We cannot tell you, amid Youth Culture 3.0, to "do it our way" (as if there were such a thing as "our way"). Any organization that tells you that is lying or seriously misguided and out of touch with teenagers today. What we *can* do, and *will* do, is serve you and resource you in the process of discerning and developing a communional, missional, not-driven-but-present youth ministry that's contextually appropriate for the teenagers in your midst and those you're called to reach.

As I've been writing this book, I've kept track of a few stories of youth workers who are wrestling with some of the ideas in this book, and I'd like to share them with you now. One is a purely emotive and cognitive rant of dissatisfaction with the way things are and the difficulty of moving toward change. Two others are unique little slices of practical experimentation. Both of these latter examples could turn out to have wonderful subsequent chapters, or they could crash and burn in a pile. But the courageous effort is glorious in itself.

First, the rant.

Joe Troyer, a youth worker in Canton, Ohio, posted this on his blog:[90]

> *I don't know what to do. This is so frustrating. What do you do when what you always did doesn't do it anymore? Youth culture and maybe culture in general has turned a corner. We talk about being "missional" and how attractional just isn't cutting it anymore. Yet traditional youth ministry is nothing but attractional. We have events and tell kids to bring their friends to us. We feel like youth ministry has to have some sense of "attractiveness." At the same time, across much of my county, youth ministries are in a lull and are bogging down. I hear it from youth pastors all the time. We think maybe we need to teach better. Or maybe we need to get some games in there to make it more exciting. Maybe we need a catchy name with words like XTREME or FIRE or XTREME FIRE! I mean it's got to be better than Hartville Mennonite Church MYF (Mennonite Youth Fellowship), right? How can we make one event more exciting than the next? I am so tired of it.*
>
> *I am tired of doing the same old stuff. Why? IT ISN'T WORKING!! Now to be intellectually honest, it is possible*

that maybe I am not that great of a youth pastor. Possible. There is always something I could be working on. But at the same time, I know God has called me here for a purpose and a reason. That reason is to love kids and point them toward the kingdom. But how? We have Sunday school. We have Bible Study. We have activities and fundraisers. I visit some kids at school. Sound familiar? Sure it does. This is how youth ministry has been done since its inception. It's broken. And I don't know how to fix it. What do we do in a postmodern, post-Christendom world? Is it unsettling to anyone else?

So what is keeping me from change? Two things: Fear and Uncertainty.

What I fear are the repercussions of change in my congregation. It's an issue of "Blowback." I fear that it will be unacceptable and seen as reckless. To put it bluntly, I am afraid of losing my job. I fear failure (whatever that means). I fear that it will be wrong and do damage. I fear that it's something that the church could not sustain. I fear that it will hurt the youth, although I am motivated out of love for them.

Uncertainty: If we don't do it this way, how the heck are we supposed to do it? There is a vast unknown out there. What shape is my youth group supposed to take on? What is it? Maybe it isn't the issue of what it's supposed to be like, but maybe it is an issue of "Core Values." Maybe we need to restructure not out of a vision statement, but out of what we value as a community. As

a lot of ministries go, we don't have a set of core values that grounds us.

Now what? It's time for change, but what? It isn't work-ing. Let's deal with it. It isn't a fad or a season. It is re-ality. We are doing youth ministry just like in the 1970s. Same old stuff in new shoes. It is time to be honest and embrace change. But where to start?

I love Joe's honesty, and you can easily see many of the themes of this book popping up in his post. I told Joe, and I'll tell you as well (whether you're a paid or volunteer youth worker, a senior pastor, or some other kind of church leader): Joe is expressing a frustration that thousands of youth work-ers are feeling and experiencing every day. If you're a youth worker in this place, then know that you're not alone and you aren't crazy. If you're a senior pastor or church leader, then take special notice of Joe's fears, which are common to most youth workers who genuinely want to bring about needed change. Please, be a supportive and grace-giving permission giver.

Now, a wonderful story of a gutsy youth worker couple and four courageous churches...

I met Seth and Crystal Dady at one of Youth Specialties' Na-tional Youth Workers Conventions. They waited patiently at the end of a seminar I'd just finished giving, called "A New Vision for Middle School Ministry," during which I'd teased some of the issues in this book. After a line of question-askers thinned out, they approached me with their question. To be honest, I don't remember the question; I only remember their story. As bits of it leaked out, I kept interrupting them to ask more.

Seth and Crystal do youth ministry in the small Colorado mountain town of Lake City. Theirs is not a perfect youth ministry, and they would never contend that it is. But it's radical and revolutionary in one huge aspect: Seth and Crystal are jointly supported by the five churches in their town. Did you catch that? Seth and Crystal are the *town youth workers*, and they were hired to lead an independent (yet, in some ways, connected to all five churches) youth ministry to reach the teenagers of Lake City.

And the mix of the five churches that hired Seth and Crystal makes it almost unbelievable: Grace Fellowship (nondenominational), First Baptist of Lake City, St. Rose of Lima Catholic, St. James Episcopal, and Community Presbyterian Church.

In many ways, their little youth ministry does the same things that many youth ministries do. But the vision is different. Seth and Crystal, supported by five churches with widely disparate beliefs, are ministering in the margins. They're sitting in the stairwell that leads to youth culture underground and building relationships with real kids—outside the walls of the church. They're building a youth ministry for and with the kids they meet, and they're growing it through the natural social networks that exist in their town.

I was stunned. In fact, I called them onstage during a general session at our convention and told their story to the 4,500 youth workers present. Seth and Crystal stood in humble tears and awe as thousands of youth workers applauded and cheered for them. The emotional sense of hope was palpable in the room, and I could almost see little thought bubbles popping up above hundreds of heads and containing the words, "If someone can do something different, then just maybe I can, too."

We want to keep Seth and Crystal around, so I gave them a huge gift certificate to get resources from our store and free registration to join us at the National Youth Workers Convention again next year. I'm now on their prayer list, and I receive regular email updates from them.

And, finally, an email exchange that I had with Kerry Snyder, a youth worker in Arizona. I'll let Kerry's email tell his story:

Thanks for opening this. I'm looking for some feedback and what you think about an idea me and my junior high pastor had today.

I'm the student ministries pastor at a church out here in AZ for the past five years. We've been in our facility for almost three years, and our church has gone from 600 when I started to 1,800 now.

As far as students go, we started with 40 from 6th–12th grade. Now we have over 200 on average each Sunday, about 80 in junior high and 130 in high school. Problem is, we've only grown in budget $3,000. Currently, we have a $12,000 budget for all of student ministries.

Each year at review, the board and other pastors glow and talk up all the work we've done on such a small budget and give us hopes of a larger budget and whatnot, but alas, it's usually the first thing to get cut.

But this email is not about our numbers or our budget frustrations. I don't mean to gripe or complain. We

have a ton of encouragement and support from our staff and board. God's definitely blessed us and brought tons of students to the ministry, and they're responding in amazing ways to God's call on their lives. We're blessed; a lot of churches don't have this many kids, this kind of response, or this much money. We've been working in Africa and Fiji. I know that they do ministry with so much less. In 13 years of ministry I've never let money dictate God's call and vision on the ministry. He's put me here. But sometimes money is a necessity; especially when we look at doing our outreaches, worship nights, and all the supplies for our experiential and responsive elements.

All that to say, today in our student ministries staff meeting, we came up with a rather interesting and experimental idea: Ministry on zero budget. We decided the $12,000 could be turned back around to our student mission movements (Vision Abolition and Vision Africa) or our community and outreach programs.

This isn't to try and prove our board "wrong" or smack them in the face. It's not a silent protest against a small budget. It's an experiment. One that, if we follow through, could be pretty impacting on our ministry and church. We've all committed to pray about this every day for two weeks and also to contact others who we respect and value the opinions of.

We've also decided to let our students truly "own" this ministry by using their giving to help support it, as well

*as us passing on what they give to organizations like
Children of the Nations, or something like that.*

*So what I'm asking for is your honest feedback on
this idea. Any thoughts, comments, ideas would be
greatly appreciated.*

I responded to Kerry with affirmation and a few words of
caution. (For instance, they should be aware that if they choose
to use their budget in this way, then it's likely that there will
be people in the church who believe their budget should really
be cut to zero.)

Kerry responded:

Marko:
*By the way, we decided to go for it. We are going to
present it to the staff and board in the next couple
weeks. We are committed to following through with this
experiment for at least a year. If it works, we hope that
we can grow it to the point where our salaries are even
taken care of. Who knows? I feel like God is calling us
to take this one on faith. It makes us be completely dependent on Him, more creative, more intentional, saying no to more while becoming more focused on the
most important thing: Christ.*

I love so much about what Kerry and his team are doing.
I love that they're taking their frustration and completely going the opposite direction than expected. I love that they went
through a process of discernment to make this decision and
didn't just write a proposal and take a vote. I love that they

expect failure, to some extent. I love that they are choosing this path because it will force them to be truly innovative and involve teenagers in the process. I love that it's a gutsy and wild experiment!

I'm sure we could find hundreds of other wonderful stories of youth workers experimenting with Youth Ministry 3.0. Problem is, the humble spirit and values of this new mindset results in early adopters who have no real interest in being identified or copied or commoditized. So most of them are faithfully operating under the radar.

My hope and dream is that we'll see a groundswell of courageous youth workers who are willing to fail, willing to risk, willing to step out in faith and passion and into a calling to reach Youth Culture 3.0 teenagers with the present and transformative love of Jesus Christ. My hope and dream is that 10 years from now, we can easily show hundreds of examples—thousands of examples—of contextual, communional, missional, present youth ministries that are living out the gospel in the real world of today's adolescents. Amen to that!

I'll close with Eugene Peterson's beautiful wording of Jesus' instructions to the disciples, from Matthew 10:9-10 (*The Message*, emphasis mine):

> *Don't think you have to put on a fund-raising*
> *campaign before you start.*
> *You don't need a lot of equipment.*
> **You are the equipment,**
> *and all you need to keep that going*
> *is three meals a day.*
> *Travel light.*

1. If you're mean-spirited enough, and you want to watch me struggle for breath...if you want to laugh at me along with my "friends" who were there that day...then you can find a link to the video at this Web address: http://www.youtube.com/watch?v=xRXgwcQdpnE.

2. The Barna Group, "Twentysomethings Struggle to Find Their Place in Christian Churches," *The Barna Update*, September 24, 2003, http://www.barna.org/FlexPage.aspx?Page=BarnaUpdate&BarnaUpdateID=149 (accessed 3/30/08).

3. LifeWay Staff, "LifeWay Research Uncovers Reasons 18 to 22 Year Olds Drop Out of Church," *LifeWay Research*, http://www.lifeway.com/lwc/article_main_page/0%2C1703%2CA%25253D165949%252526M%25253D200906%2C00.html? (accessed 3/30/08). While the research reports a number of 70 percent, it's stated this way: "A new study from LifeWay Research reveals that more than two-thirds of young adults who attend a Protestant church for at least a year in high school will stop regularly attending church for at least a year between the ages of 18 and 22." This means that a teenager who was involved in youth group for a year in ninth grade but stopped coming would still be included as a "dropout,"

which is different than a student who went through a youth ministry all four years and then stopped attending church. This fact and other surveys (such as the Barna research in the previous note and similar research done by the Gallup organization) would lend credibility to a dropout percentage closer to 50 percent.

4. In *Soul Searching: The Religious and Spiritual Lives of American Teenagers* (Oxford University Press, 2005), authors Christian Smith and Melinda Lundquist Denton "suggest that the de facto dominant religion among contemporary U.S. teenagers is what we might well call 'Moralistic Therapeutic Deism.' The creed of this religion, as codified from what emerged from our interviews, sounds something like this:

1. A God exists who created and orders the world and watches over human life on earth.
2. God wants people to be good, nice, and fair to each other, as taught in the Bible and by most world religions.
3. The central goal of life is to be happy and to feel good about oneself.
4. God does not need to be particularly involved in one's life except when God is needed to resolve a problem.
5. Good people go to heaven when they die." (pp. 162–163)

5. At the time of this writing, you can view the "Wendy's Hole" commercial on YouTube at www.youtube.com/watch?v=9Qd5UEfs4W8.

6. Jon Savage has written an excellent and helpful (although extremely lengthy) book for anyone who really wants to understand the cultural phenomenon that is youth culture. The book is called *Teenage: The Creation of Youth Culture* (Viking, 2007). In it he traces the cultural movements and organizations for youth, starting with the mid-1800s and on through the end of World War II when youth culture became a widely acknowledged subculture both in North America and in Europe.

7. *Adolescence: Its Psychology and Its Relations to Physiology, Anthropology, Sociology, Sex, Crime, and Religion* (Appleton, 1904). I've heard people say (and have said it myself) that Hall coined the term *adolescence*. This isn't the case. The term existed, it seems, for a few hundred years prior to Hall. But, certainly, Hall was the one who popularized the word, and it was the first time that most people had heard it (which is likely why many people believe he made it up).

8. Hall was a staunch evolutionist and banner carrier of Darwinism. The connections, I believe, are clear: Because his mindset was already committed to evolution, Hall was able to see culture as evolving and changing. This allowed him to consider the "rise" of a new phenomenon within shifting culture.

9. Hall's notion of "Storm and Stress" (and the three key elements) was popular for a few decades, but then it fell out of style with those who studied, spoke, and wrote about adolescents. In recent years, the notion has seen a bit of resurgence, but not as a universal experience or a way to describe adoles-

cence. Even those who believe it's close to universal explain that it could be a very quick blip for some teenagers. For a bit more on this, read the Wikipedia article on G. Stanley Hall: http://en.wikipedia.org/wiki/G._Stanley_Hall.

10. These three issues shouldn't be confused with the three key elements of "storm and stress," as described by Hall.

11. Researchers who study the onset of puberty pretty much always study girls. There are a couple reasons for this. First, while girls officially show signs of puberty with the growth of breast buds and pubic hair, menarche (their first period) is a widely accepted marker. These markers are all visible. And girls—throughout the ages—have been willing to talk about their first periods (at least with people they trust). The start of puberty for boys is less obvious and less agreed upon. Some say it's a boy's first nocturnal emission. Other people have different definitions. Either way, boys don't talk about it. In fact, boys lie about it. So researchers study girls. We do know that boys tend to follow about a year or a year and a half behind girls in puberty and other adolescent development realities.

12. There are plenty of other factors that play into the rise of a greater focus on youth culture, such as our cultural obsession with youth, the role of teenage and young adult celebrities, the increased buying power of teenagers (which, as I wrote earlier, creates a cyclical effect of companies spending millions on marketing to teenage buyers), and more. But I've often seen this "sheer number factor" due to the expansion of adolescence get overlooked.

13. This number is hotly debated. I find it intriguing that people get so passionate about disagreeing with the research on this. Really, the tone of voice when people express their skepticism can only be described as "threatened." I'm not completely sure what they're threatened by. A generous possibility is that they're hoping to protect the childhood years from being absconded into adolescence (a trend that—puberty aside—seems to be propelled by marketing to preteens and "tweens"). When I cite these numbers, I'm often asked (sometimes by a skeptic, sometimes by someone who's merely interested and not disagreeing) for references to studies backing this up. While I've included these endnotes, this book is certainly not a truly academic book (duh!), and I'll not fully support my claim other than to say the numbers have been shown over and over again in various studies. I will cite a few of them, if merely to allow us to move on:

Marcia E. Herman-Giddens, Eric J. Slora, Richard C. Wasserman, Carlos J. Bourdony, Manju V. Bhapkar, Gary G. Koch, and Cynthia M. Hasemeier. "Secondary Sexual Characteristics and Menses in Young Girls Seen in Office Practice: A Study from the Pediatric Research in Office Settings Network," *Pediatrics* 99, (April 1997): 505–512. http://pediatrics.aappublications.org/cgi/content/abstract/99/4/505 (accessed 3/30/08).

Diana Zuckerman Ph.D., "When Little Girls Become Women: Early Onset of Puberty in Girls," National Research Center for Women & Families—Children's Health, http://www.center4research.org/children11.html (accessed 3/30/08).

P.B. Kaplowitz, S.E. Oberfield, and the Drug and Therapeutics and Executive Committees of the Lawson Wilkins Pediatric Endocrine Society, "Re-examination of the Age Limit for Defining When Puberty Is Precocious in Girls in the United States," *Pediatrics* 104, (October 1999): 936–941. http://pediatrics.aappublications. org/cgi/content/full/104/4/936?ijkey=51a3e30c7ef6635 6541e2f346991c5cc9300baf7 (accessed 3/30/08).

14. The other question that's interesting to people in this "age drop of puberty" issue is "Why?" For years, there were three competing theories: Some thought it was due to hormones, preservatives, and other additives in our diet; others thought it was due to a more well-rounded diet (compared to people who lived hundreds of years ago); and still others hypothesized that the drop was a physiological response to the cultural pressure on kids to act older at younger and younger ages. But in recent years, the first of those theories (hormones, additives, and preservatives in our food) seems to have won the day, both in research and popular opinion.

15. Connect this with aging baby boomers' desire to hold on to aspects of their adolescence, and a wad of new sociological results show up, such as the disappearance of the generation gap, the dominance of youth culture in setting trends, the commoditization of adolescent celebrities, and (when coupled with the rise of the Internet and instant, free access to information) the rise of a global youth culture.

16. Dictionary.com (http://dictionary.reference.com/browse/identity)

17. TheFreeDictionary.com (http://www.thefreedictionary.com/identity)

18. Cambridge Advanced Learner's Dictionary (http://dictionary.cambridge.org/define.asp?key=38918&dict=CALD)

19. Chap Clark, in his reading of this manuscript, sent me a helpful and thoughtful comment on these developmental tasks, which I'll share here as a direct quote: "You clearly nod to traditional developmental psychology thinking, yet both theologically (Psalm 139, for example) and in some developmental circles, the real quest is 'spiritual discovery,' meaning that God has created each one unique, with a specific gifting, calling, and person. *Formation* does not align with a robust theology of creation or redemption." Chap's comment deserves more thinking on my part and yours. Good stuff!

20. To be clear, this shift into and acquisition of abstract thinking is a multiyear process, taking most of the adolescent years. With the lengthening of adolescence, some have started talking about adolescence as having three distinct phases: Early (or young) adolescence, midadolescence, and late adolescence (or what Jeffery J. Arnett is pushing to call "emerging adulthood"). The "abilities" that come with abstract thinking not only implicate cognition and process, but also worldview and relationships. Midadolescents are said to move through a period some are calling "egocentric abstraction." Chap Clark says, "Due to the lengthening of adolescence in late modernity, from approximately 15 to 19 [years old], identity and autonomy feel so distant and untenable, the midadolescent feels like they must do whatever it takes to protect themselves."

21. Recent research has shown that the part of the human brain most responsible for many of these abstract functions—particularly hypothesizing, speculation, decision-making, and all functions related to wisdom—is underdeveloped in teenagers and not fully formed (physiologically speaking) until the mid-20s. There's still a good amount of debate on this, as the findings are so new, but the implications seem to be that teenagers gain this new abstract thinking ability at puberty. They wrestle with putting it into use not only because of inexperience, but also because their brains haven't finished developing yet. In other words, there's a biological explanation for why teenagers are so slow to "get" some of this stuff, and why they're so notorious for poor decision-making, poor prioritization, and a general lack of wisdom. For more on this, read the excellent book *The Primal Teen* by Barbara Strauch (Doubleday, 2003).

22. Psychological literature calls this an "imaginary audience."

23. From personal correspondence with Chap Clark, April 2008.

24. Thanks to Dr. Marv Penner for this addition.

25. Instead of referring to this as "separate selves," some are now referring to this reality as "layers," suggesting that in each of these situations, my daughter is living out three different yet authentic selves.

26. This is going to be anything but an academic history of youth ministry. Really, for a full history of youth ministry, one has to go back a lot further than the 1950s. I'm starting

there because I consider it the advent of what I'm calling "the modern youth ministry movement"—which is to say, youth ministry that exists in response to a universally accepted youth culture. Mark Senter has a reasonably good history of youth ministry (going further back) in his currently out-of-print (but still easy to find) book, *The Coming Revolution in Youth Ministry* (Victor Books, 1992). The rumor is that Senter is writing a full-length history of youth ministry, so watch for that. I found Jon Savage's *Teenage: The Creation of Youth Culture* (Viking, 2007) extremely helpful in understanding the societal movements prior to World War II that set the stage for modern youth culture. Savage traces youth movements in North America and Europe from the mid-1800s through the end of World War II.

27. Again, see Jon Savage's *Teenage: The Creation of Youth Culture* for a 500-page treatment of this. On one hand, reading this book gave me much more information than I needed, but on the other hand, it really provided me with a deeper understanding of the tidal swell toward an acknowledged youth culture.

28. An absolutely critical factor here that shouldn't be missed is the rise of the American high school. Late in the 1940s, for the first time in the history of...well...the earth, there were more teenagers in high school than not in high school. This growth continued through the '50s until high school attendance became both mandatory and completely the norm. High schools became a Petri dish for the explosion of youth culture, providing a "place" that hadn't existed prior.

29. Read a short summary of Youth for Christ's history on this page of their Web site: http://www.yfc.net/Brix?pageID=12575 (accessed April 9, 2008).

30. To be fair, Young Life got its start before World War II and pioneered many of the "club" aspects I attribute to Youth Ministry 2.0 thinking and practice. For a brief summary of Young Life's history, see this page on their Web site: http://www.younglife.org/AboutYoungLife/History.htm (accessed April 9, 2008).

31. I'm sure something could be said here about the sociology or psychology of this. Most of the earliest Christian youth workers were evangelists at heart. They brought their spiritual gifting and passion to their work with teenagers. So it might be a bit false to simply state that youth culture called for evangelists at this point, as there's likely a chicken-and-egg thing going on.

32. Again, to be fair, this condescension to the "other" culture was commonplace in missions practice at the time.

33. Kenda Dean, "The New Rhetoric of Youth Ministry," *Journal of Youth and Theology* 2, no. 2 (November 2003), 9.

34. Kenda Dean, "The New Rhetoric of Youth Ministry," *Journal of Youth and Theology* 2, no. 2 (November 2003); Kenda Dean, *Youth Ministry as the Transformation of Passion: A Practical Theological Analysis of Youth and Their Ministry to American Mainline Protestantism* (Ph.D. dissertation for Princeton Theological Seminary, 1996); and email correspon-

dence with Dr. Kenda Dean, March and April, 2008.

35. Andy was a doctoral student of Kenda Dean's at Princeton, and he fleshes out his ideas in his thesis-turned-book, *Revisiting Relational Youth Ministry: From a Strategy of Influence to a Theology of Incarnation* (IVP Books, 2007).

36. Of course at this time most youth pastors were barely post-youth themselves, and they saw youth ministry as a path to other (read: more important) roles in pastoral ministry. Churches saw youth pastors as "junior pastors" or "pastors in training," and it was generally assumed that a youth pastor would stay for only a few years before growing up into a "real" ministry job.

37. Props to the church I grew up in, Ward Presbyterian Church, then in Livonia, Michigan, for being extremely revolutionary in hiring a full-time junior high pastor in the second half of the '70s, when it was almost unheard of to have such a staff position.

38. A funny story: Shortly after selling out their "first press run" of Ideas books, Mike and Wayne stood at the counter of the county recorder in San Diego to register their new business. The clerk asked them for the name of the organization, and they looked at each other and realized they'd forgotten to think about that one little detail. The story goes that Mike said to Wayne, "What should we call it?" Wayne answered, "I don't know. I've got a 'Corvette Specialties' by my house—how 'bout we call it 'Youth Specialties'?" And that was it. A small processing fee and minutes later, Youth Specialties was stuck with a name that has, luckily, worked out okay

for four decades. We're just glad Wayne didn't think of the Pancake Palace near his house, or we'd be saddled with a horrible name.

39. As noted earlier, this has as much to do with spending power and big business as anything else. Marketers realized there was fruit ripe for the picking and began creating thousands of products for teenagers, as well as marketing non-youth specific products in youth-y ways. Teenagers' unquenchable thirst for their own music led to the enormous growth of the recording industry in the explosive genres of rock, pop, and R&B. Alongside this, radio stations geared toward youth multiplied in number, and movies specifically targeting teenagers were the rage. Books were published for a teenage reader. In fact, for the first time, these books were truly written for the teenage consumer, not just adults who had something to say to "those darn kids."

40. One needs only to look at any one of dozens (or hundreds) of youth culture aspects to see this. But let's take an easy one: Music. Whenever a genre of music that's previously been a youth-only domain (i.e., adults say, "I just don't understand that noise!") becomes mainstream, new genres and subgenres spring up to redefine the edges. When everyone's parents were also listening to rock music, "alternative rock" sprang up. The word *alternative* combined with *rock* doesn't mean a thing today, as it's now become mainstream. So other subgenres sprang up. Let's use emo as an example. At first, emo was widely misunderstood by adults, which kept it as the wonderful little private domain of teenagers. But now emo is becoming mainstream, and adults are buying up Death Cab

for Cutie albums as much as teenagers are. So emo had to subdivide into a few dozen new subgenres, just to provide a new "teen-only club."

41. This is not a book on church culture in general, so I won't go into lots of detail here. But a quick perusal of the following reveals the love we had for systemization from the 1970s through the 1990s: The Four Spiritual Laws, Evangelism Explosion ("If you were to die tonight…"), Willow Creek, Saddleback, church growth seminars, The One-Minute Pastor, and a host of others. Many of these (Willow Creek and Saddleback among them) have moved beyond the "come learn to do it our way" approach of that era. Others on this list have stood their ground and become close to obsolete.

42. During this era, evangelism in youth ministry got relegated, primarily, to the parachurch youth ministry organizations that really came into their own identity alongside (and sometimes in competition with) the church.

43. This "success=quantity" formula is straight from the evil one, and it permeates many, if not most, of our churches. It's so much a part of our thinking now that it's almost impossible to think differently. I'm passionate about not being impressed by numbers, but when a friend recently shared with me (in humility, to be fair to him) that he had more than 800 junior highers attend his winter retreat, I couldn't help myself: I was über-impressed! I *assumed* it must be good. I *assumed* it should be copied. Now, numbers *do* mean something. They just don't always mean things are good or right. If a youth group jumps from 12 kids to 40 kids, then it should be noticed

and questions should be asked: "Is it because we're providing a safe and loving place for kids? Or is it because we're putting on a really good show?" Likewise, if a group slowly drops from 40 kids to 12 kids, then different questions should be asked: "Is it because we're irrelevant or unsafe or exclusive? Or is it because we've decided to stop merely entertaining kids and giving out really cool door prizes?"

44. At the time of this writing, this video (called "Louisiana State Employees") can be seen on YouTube at http://www.youtube.com/watch?v=e0SfpH2AFdk.

45. Of course, these are the youth pastor's thoughts. The church's response is often, *We need a new youth pastor!*

46. Yeah, I know "the previous millennium" was only a few years ago; but it's a cool coincidence that it happens to be true!

47. As quoted in *The Shaping of Things to Come* by Michael Frost and Alan Hirsch (Hendrickson, 2003), vi.

48. Resource Interactive, "Decoding the Digital Millennials: Large in Number, Huge in Influence," *Litmus*, November 2006, 3, http://www.resource.com/adx/aspx/adxgetmedia.aspx?MediaID=654 (accessed 3/30/08). Key quote from this study: "[digital millennials] should be viewed as co-purchasers for nearly everything purchased within a household, from 81% of apparel and 52% of vehicles (Harris Interactive, 2006)."

49. Case in point: My 14-year-old daughter has recently been moving out of her pop/R&B listening exclusivity and choos-

ing music with a harder edge. She raided my iTunes and is now a huge fan of My Chemical Romance, Chris Cornell, Audioslave, Death Cab for Cutie, Arctic Monkeys, Beck, and a host of other music that *she got from me!* My musical diet is still dramatically wider than hers, but we don't fight over the radio station in the car anymore.

50. For more on this "going underground" phenomenon, and especially the pain in teenagers' lives that drives them there, see Dr. Chap Clark's fantastic and insightful book *Hurt: Inside the World of Today's Teenagers* (Baker Academic, 2004).

51. If the underground/subterranean metaphor isn't working for you and makes you think of a *literal* underground, then think of this facet of adolescent culture as hidden instead.

52. Of course, this is a generalization. Spot-on true in many, if not most, schools; metaphorically true in all of them.

53. Molly Steenson, "What Is Burning Man?" *The Experience*, http://www.burningman.com/whatisburningman/about_burningman/experience.html (accessed 3/30/08).

54. While I'm using the metaphor of cultural anthropology, my friend Tim Keel astutely develops the metaphor of leaders as environmentalists in his excellent book *Intuitive Leadership* (Baker Books, 2007). Here's a great short paragraph from Tim's book: "Do you see yourself as a leader who is cultivating an environment or as an administrator running programs? How are we cultivating life in our communities? I believe that churches need leaders who are environmentalists. Environ-

mentalists can help to shape the relational and spiritual ecologies that generate life as the natural outgrowth of a healthy and dynamic ecosystem" (page 242).

55. It's not that evangelism should cease to exist! Far from it. But the methods and assumptions surrounding evangelism in Youth Ministry 1.0 aren't workable, for the most part, in today's youth culture. So, yes, evangelism still exists; but it's radically reshaped by our new assumptions, understandings, and approaches.

56. Similar to the previous note, discipleship and creating a positive peer group don't go away; they just get radically reframed. And one-size-fits-all discipleship unfortunately (because it was easier, whether or not it was effective) needs to be framed on the wall of our youth ministry history museum and left behind.

57. Please tell me you've read Bonhoeffer's *Life Together.* If not, or if you haven't read it in the past few years, then put this book down and go read it!

58. Scott Miller's blog: http://www.catholicymblog.com/

59. Michael Frost and Alan Hirsch, *The Shaping of Things to Come* (Peabody, MA: Hendrickson, 2003), xi.

60. In his excellent book *The New Christians: Dispatches from the Emergent Frontier* (Jossey-Bass, 2008), Tony Jones has much to say to put flesh on this theme.

61. I asked for help on these words in a blog post and was soon sent 70 of the best comments I've ever received on my blog. Particular thanks go to the following commenters for their shaping input: D. Scott Miller, Chad Swanzy, Joe Troyer, Adam Lehman, Len Evans, Gordon Weir, Tammy Klassen, Jay Phillippi, Natalie Stadnick, Grahame Knox, Dustin Perkins, Sue Van Stelle, Bob Carlton, Tash McGill, Liz Graves, Tammy Harris, Mark Riddle, Robin Dugall, Daniel So, Jodi Shay.

62. Though I didn't intentionally draw from Mike King's book, *Presence-Centered Youth Ministry*, I'm sure it informed my thinking on this, even if only in its title. Mark Yaconelli's groundbreaking book *Contemplative Youth Ministry* (Zondervan/Youth Specialties, 2006) also discusses these themes at length.

63. http://www.dfj.com/J, used with permission.

64. Remember, even seemingly insignificant choices such as what food to eat, what clothes to wear, and what music to listen to have meaning. They all have values behind them.

65. In his excellent book *Intuitive Leadership: Embracing a Paradigm of Narrative, Metaphor, and Chaos* (Baker Books, 2007), Tim Keel devotes a full third of the book to the idea and practice of contextualization. I highly recommend this book to any leader interested in learning more about the practice of contextualization in a postmodern framework.

66. The hopeful exception to this is if the 200 or so schools represented in the Youth Specialties Academic Support

Network (http://www.youthspecialties.com/academic/ysasn/)—
all of whom have a major or minor in youth ministry—would
truly prepare students as cultural anthropologists rather than
merely preparing them to run programs. (Some of them do
this, but not enough of them.)

67. Mark Yaconelli has much to say about this discerning process in his book *Contemplative Youth Ministry* (Zondervan/
Youth Specialties, 2006).

68. "Swarming" is a quirky twenty-first-century phenomenon
in which social networks all communicate a place and time,
under the radar of any official marketing effort or promotion,
to show up and do something together. At first, these were
primarily stunts: 100 people would show up in front of city
hall and stand facing the other direction, or 60 people would
suddenly materialize in a subway station and sing the same
song. It was done for kicks or to make a point. But swarming has evolved into an intentionally low-budget, low-flash,
high-relationship means of gathering a group through natural
relational lines (usually via text messaging). I know of one
church that meets almost exclusively via swarming.

69. *Glocal* is a word used by many to talk about the shift
in place-identity in a postmodern context. In modern times
(and, for our purposes, we might say in the first two epochs of
youth culture), people's identities were fixed, geographically,
at the national and individual levels. Postmoderns talk about
identity being fixed, nongeographically, at the global and local
levels. *Global* and *local* combine into the mashup word *glocal*:
"I'm a citizen of the world and rooted in a local community."

70. Chap Clark makes this point strongly, with extensive examples and history, in his book *Hurt: Inside the World of Today's Teenagers* (Baker Academic, 2004).

71. Pete Ward, a noted youth ministry academic in the UK, is known for saying there are only two kinds of youth ministries: Inward-facing and outward-facing. While I believe this is overly simplistic, the wording (and the mental maps it provides) is helpful.

72. Martin writes in his autobiography, *Born Standing Up: A Comic's Life* (Scribner, 2007, p. 117), that this was one of the earliest "lines" that started to move him out of traditional comedy (and magic!) into the brand of zaniness that set him on his explosive path to performing in stadiums in front of thousands.

73. Yes, some small groups (both for youth and adults) grow to supercede these negative stereotypes. My contention would be that most small groups that truly move beyond those stereotypes really begin to function as house churches (or, in a youth ministry context, as mini youth groups).

74. Doug Pagitt, in his provocative book *A Christianity Worth Believing* (Jossey-Bass, 2008), describes how a well-meaning discipler drew this for him on a restaurant placemat two weeks after Doug's conversion. Doug folded it up and kept it in his wallet for 20 years or so, before finally scanning it into his computer. It didn't seem right to Doug from the get-go, but he originally tried to live into the suggestions of the diagram. Eventually, Doug kept the diagram to remind himself of

the change that had occurred in the shift from modernism to postmodernism.

75. Many have done a much better job of explaining this shift than I am either capable of or will attempt to do in this small space. If you'd like to read more, a good starting point is the opening chapters of Dan Kimball's book *The Emerging Church* (Zondervan, 2003).

76. To reveal my cards, in case they're not already obvious, I believe it's useless to think of modernism as bad and postmodernism as good (or vice versa). Both are neutral, in a sense; or, more accurately, both have good sides and ugly sides. Modernism was wrongly obsessed with finality, false conclusion and confidence, systemization, mechanization, and a host of other problematic issues (particularly when they saturated our theology and ministry values). Postmodernism has challenges also, of course; but I believe it provides us with some wonderful opportunities: Not being in competition with science, faith allowed to be faith (and not something that has to be proven), a dialogical approach rather than a combative approach, a willingness to ask hard questions and not rush to simplistic answers, and more.

77. Of course, "Be in the world, but not of it" isn't actually a verse in the Bible (which might be a surprise to many who quote it as if it were!). It's a theological phrase representing a cobbling together of several scriptural themes. Some biblical references that speak to this are John 17:14—"I have given them your word and the world has hated them, for they are not of the world any more than I am of the world"; 2 Corin-

thians 10:2-4—"I beg you that when I come I may not have to be as bold as I expect to be toward some people who think that we live by the standards of this world. For though we live in the world, we do not wage war as the world does. The weapons we fight with are not the weapons of the world. On the contrary, they have divine power to demolish strongholds"; and 1 John 2:15-16—"Do not love the world or anything in the world. If you love the world, love for the Father is not in you. For everything in the world—the cravings of sinful people, the lust of their eyes and their boasting about what they have and do—comes not from the Father but from the world."

Shockingly, this non-verse is often used, in arguments over the evils of postmodernism, to suggest that we should not be "of" postmodernism but should be "of" modernism. What a ludicrous notion! Being "not of it" refers to our identity as created beings and our "otherness," collectively, as spiritual beings whose primary affinity is to the kingdom of God. Clearly, the examples of Jesus and Paul are ones of *engagement with* the culture in which they found themselves.

78. Yes, there are times when we need to help teenagers understand that what they see as a positive, trustworthy experience is not the whole picture and, therefore, not fully trustworthy. For example, it's likely that a teenage boy who's sexually active really enjoys sex and would naturally conclude that this experience (and the emotions that ride along with it) are trustworthy and should continue to inform his choices. We have a role in helping that boy understand that the experience is good, in a sense, because God made us sexual beings and made us to enjoy sex; but, of course, we

have a broader view that helps us understand some things that a teenage boy isn't able to see in the moment: That his sexual experience can lead to all sorts of pain and problems that aren't what God desires for him, ultimately, because of God's great love for him.

79. Someone needs to write a book for church leaders with this title! *Organic Fruit: Cultivating Pesticide-Free, Growth Hormone-Free, Natural Communion in Your Church.*

80. I use *technology* here to refer to programs and systems. Certainly, much of what teenagers will experience in communion will be supported by the online technologies of the day.

81. I love this "word," and I've been borrowing it from Anne Lamott's writing for years.

82. Bruce Olson, *Bruchko: The Astonishing True Story of a 19-Year-Old American—His Capture by the Motilone Indians and His Adventures in Christianizing the Stone Age Tribe* (1977; repr., Lake Mary, FL: Charisma House, 2006).

83. Don Richardson, *Peace Child* (Seattle: YWAM, 2007).

84. *Disequilibration* is the psychological term for being cognitively or emotionally off-balance when an experience or concept jars us out of what we assumed was true to an in-between place prior to a new understanding.

85. Peter Senge, C. Otto Scharmer, Joseph Jaworski, and Betty Sue Flowers, *Presence: Human Purpose and the Field of the*

Future (Cambridge, MA: Society for Organizational Learning, 2004; New York: Doubleday Business, 2008). The discussion of "the U" is found on pages 83-92 and 219-240, with a full diagram on page 225. (Note: The page numbers are from the 2004 edition.)

86. Used with permission, from Peter Senge, C. Otto Scharmer, Joseph Jaworski, and Betty Sue Flowers, *Presence: Human Purpose and the Field of the Future* (Cambridge, MA: Society for Organizational Learning, 2004; New York: Doubleday Business, 2008), page 225.

87. I'm building this semi-fictitious case study based on a real ministry of real teenagers from the church I attend, Journey Community Church in La Mesa, California. "Hope for the Homeless" began as a small affinity group of high school students and one middle-aged adult leader who wanted to provide some consistent friendship in the lives of San Diego's homeless. At the time of this writing, they've made sandwiches and brought them to their friends for about 250 consecutive Friday nights in a row—without missing a single week. This consistency is what's been so powerful for the homeless— and so revolutionary for the lives of these teenagers (and now young adults). They're in true relationship with homeless people. They know them by name (and are known by name). They know each other's stories. They sit and talk, they linger, they listen. They run book clubs and all kinds of other dignity-affirming initiatives with their homeless friends. Hope for the Homeless is a wonderful example of Youth Ministry 3.0: It's communal and missional, fluid yet consistent. The students who are involved have had, and continue to have,

their lives and priorities rearranged. And it's very much under the radar and built on word of mouth and natural social networks of the teenagers involved. They don't have a budget or a ministry Web site, and they're never mentioned in our church bulletin. In fact, if it weren't for the fact that I know some of the teenagers involved, I might not be aware that this amazing ministry is happening out of my own church. Hope for the Homeless is organic, and it's bearing organic fruit in the lives of the teenage participants and the homeless friends they serve. To see a video of some of the students involved in this ministry, which clearly illustrates the stages of "the U" that I write about in this section, check out the Youth Specialties section of YouTube: http://www.youtube.com/watch?v=XKYpk-lKEwA (accessed April 2008).

88. Deuteronomy 10:14; Psalm 24:1

89. I'm sure some would say we can be "driven by our passion." And while I can't completely disagree with that (and this probably becomes a matter of semantics), I don't think I believe that anymore. I think passion pulls and invites us rather than drives us.

90. Joe has shut down his blog, so there is no active link to this post.

SUGGESTED READING

Bonhoeffer, Dietrich. *Life Together: A Discussion of Christian Fellowship*. New York: Harper & Row, 1954.

Clark, Chap. *Hurt: Inside the World of Today's Teenagers*. Grand Rapids, MI: Baker Academic, 2004.

Frost, Michael, and Alan Hirsch. *The Shaping of Things to Come: Innovation and Mission for the 21st-Century Church*. Peabody, MA: Hendrickson, 2003.

Goodstein, Anastasia. Ypulse—a blog containing daily news and commentary about generation Y for media and marketing professionals, founded in May 2004, http://www.ypulse.com.

Hall, G. Stanley. *Adolescence: Its Psychology and Its Relations to Physiology, Anthropology, Sociology, Sex, Crime, and Religion*. New York: Appleton, 1904.

Jones, Tony. *The New Christians: Dispatches from the Emergent Frontier*. San Francisco: Jossey-Bass, 2008.

Keel, Tim. *Intuitive Leadership: Embracing a Paradigm of Narrative, Metaphor, and Chaos*. Grand Rapids, MI: Baker Books, 2007.

Kimball, Dan. *The Emerging Church: Vintage Christianity for New Generations.* Forewords by Rick Warren and Brian McLaren. Grand Rapids, MI: Zondervan, 2003.

King, Mike. *Presence-Centered Youth Ministry: Guiding Students into Spiritual Formation.* Downers Grove, IL: InterVarsity Press, 2006.

Noxon, Christopher. *Rejuvenile: Kickball, Cartoons, Cupcakes, and the Reinvention of the American Grown-up.* New York: Crown, 2006.

Pagitt, Doug. *A Christianity Worth Believing: Hope-Filled, Open-Armed, Alive-And-Well Faith for the Left Out, Left Behind, and Let Down in Us All.* San Francisco: Jossey-Bass, 2008.

Savage, Jon. *Teenage: The Creation of Youth Culture.* New York: Viking, 2007.

Senge, Peter, C. Otto Scharmer, Joseph Jaworski, and Betty Sue Flowers. *Presence: Human Purpose and the Field of the Future.* Cambridge, MA: Society for Organizational Learning, 2004; New York: Doubleday Business, 2008.

Senter, Mark III. *The Coming Revolution in Youth Ministry.* Wheaton, IL: Victor Books, 1992.

Smith, Christian, and Melinda Lundquist Denton. *Soul Searching: The Religious and Spiritual Lives of American Teenagers.* New York: Oxford University Press, 2005.

Strauch, Barbara. *The Primal Teen: What the New Discoveries About the Teenage Brain Tell Us About Our Kids.* New York: Doubleday, 2003.

Yaconelli, Mark. *Contemplative Youth Ministry: Practicing the Presence of Jesus.* Grand Rapids, MI: Zondervan/Youth Specialties, 2006.